MAN
OF THE
HOUSE

Scenes from a '50s Childhood

Mark Vinz

MAN OF THE HOUSE

Scenes from a '50s Childhood

Mark Vinz

Headwaters Series

n RIVERS e PRESS w MSUM

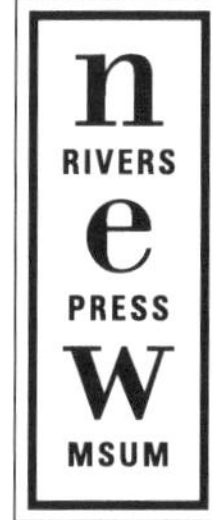

© 2017 by Mark Vinz
First Edition
Library of Congress Control Number: 2016960012
ISBN: 978-0-89823-362-9
eISBN: 978-0-89823-363-6

Cover and interior design by Mandi Wahl
Author photo by Betsy Vinz

The publication of *Man of the House* is made possible by the generous support of Minnesota State University Moorhead, the Dawson Family Endowment, and other contributors to New Rivers Press.

For copyright permission, please contact Frederick T. Courtwright at 570-839-7477 or permdude@eclipse.net.

New Rivers Press is a nonprofit literary press associated with Minnesota State University Moorhead.

Nayt Rundquist, Managing Editor
Kevin Carollo, Editor, MVP Poetry Coordinator
Travis Dolence, Director
Robert Alexander, Headwaters Series Editor
George McCormack, MVP Prose Coordinator
Thomas Anstadt, Co-Art Director
Trista Conzemius, Co-Art Director
Thom Tammaro, Poetry Editor
Alan Davis, Editor Emeritus

Publishing Interns:
Laura Grimm, Anna Landsverk, Mikaila Norman

 Printed in the USA on acid-free, archival-grade paper.

Man of the House is distributed nationally by Small Press Distribution.

 New Rivers Press
c/o MSUM
1104 7th Ave S
Moorhead, MN 56563
www.newriverspress.com

Editor's Note

Here, at long last, is Mark Vinz's magnum opus, *Man of the House*, with which New Rivers Press is pleased to introduce a new incarnation of the Headwaters Series. I became associated with the Press when Bill Truesdale acquired my first book in the early nineties, and even then Mark's manuscript was a topic of Bill's conversation. He had published a few early pieces of it in Mark's book, *The Weird Kid*, an MVP winner back in 1983, and more appeared in *Late Night Calls* a few years later, when Bill asked me to sit on the New Rivers board of directors. But for many years after that, Bill used to speak longingly of the whole manuscript—how he would ask Mark to submit the whole thing, but Mark kept telling him it was still a work in progress. "Later," he told Bill, "all things in due time."

Well, that time has come. The Headwaters Series first saw the light of day in 2000, with the publication of a single book of fiction (*The Hunger Bone*, by Deb Marquart) and one of poetry (*Red Cross Dog*, by Patricia Zontelli), but then it went into an extended period of hibernation when New Rivers moved north to Moorhead. A couple of years ago, NRP editor Al Davis and I were talking at AWP, and we decided that it might be a good time for it to rise again. I immediately thought of Mark's elusive manuscript. I think it's fitting that we decided to reinitiate the series with a book that has such a long history with the press, and with an author who served the press longer than any other member of the board. So here, kind reader, without further ado, is Mark Vinz's long-sought-after masterpiece.

Robert Alexander
Series Editor

Author's Preface

A few of these pieces centering on the two Minneapolis neighborhoods where I grew up have a fairly long history. The first were written as prose poems in the 80s and became a section called "Bergy & Me" in my book *Late Night Calls: Prose Poems and Short Fiction* (New Rivers Press, 1992). During the years since then, I've continued occasionally to work on childhood pieces, publishing several, sometimes as lyric poems or personal essays as well as prose poems, and sometimes a bit different from what has ended up in this book. Eventually, I found I'd expanded the original collection by well over a hundred entries.

As for how to classify these pieces, most of what I've written really did happen. All in all, there's very little conscious fictionalizing—mainly in changing some of the names, in the character of Bergy (who is a composite of a couple of early childhood friends), and perhaps in a few of the incidents which, as happens so often with stories, inevitably are embroidered and even reshaped by recollection or retelling. As Patricia Hampl states so well in her essay "Memory and Imagination," "memory inevitably leads to invention," and, "We must live with a version that attaches us to our limitations, to the inevitable subjectivity of our points of view."

Finally, for a number of years my chosen genres for writing have been the poem, the prose poem, the short story, and short essay, so perhaps the only way I could finally manage a memoir was to write it in short bursts—another of those subjective limitations. And here I need to specifically acknowledge Charlie Peterson, my good friend since sixth grade, who also appears in several of these pieces as Pete, and the late Keith Gunderson, whose wonderful prose poems of childhood served not only as inspiration but as models for what I wanted to do in my own work.

More than anything, I'm grateful the writing did get done, for sympathetic editors, and for all the advice and encouragement I've had along the way, no matter what its source—but especially from Robert Alexander, and from the late C. W. (Bill) Truesdale, to whom this collection is affectionately dedicated. And to my parents and sister, of course, who understood me far more than I could ever realize as a child, and to Betsy, Katie, and Sarah, my beloved family: I still may be the man of the house, but I'm also still a bit bewildered by the fairer, more complicated sex.

Mark Vinz

Contents

BOND
STAMP
SAVERS
BOOK

ONLY 1200 STAMPS
FILL THIS

QUICK
SAVER
BOOK

THE SPERRY AND HUTCHINSON COMPANY

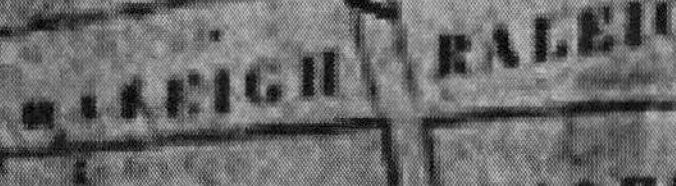

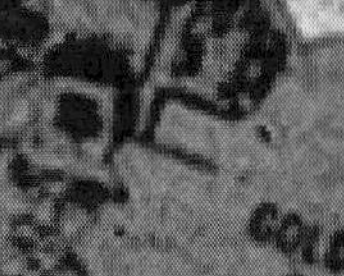

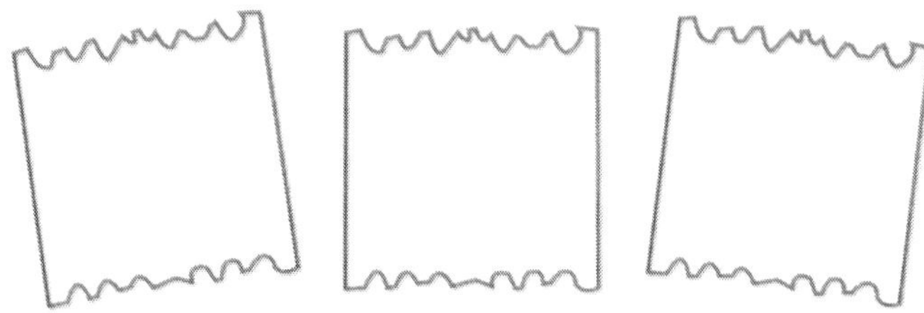

When Your Father Gets Home

It begins with a child running as fast as he can on a spring afternoon just before suppertime. I had done something wrong—who knows what it was? I was always doing something wrong, like not eating my food, not cleaning my room, not coming when I was called, and even forgetting to turn off the car radio and killing the battery. Of course, I was too small to understand such things as car batteries when my friend Bergy and I played in my father's car in the garage, pretending we were grown-up men, turning the big wheel and listening to bouncy music on the radio. In that old black Ford you didn't need to turn on the ignition to listen to the radio, but we didn't understand about ignitions either.

It begins with me running and a man running. If I had done something truly bad, I never would have run. Perhaps it was as simple as liver for supper, and I ran because there seemed nothing else to do, because I hated liver most of all the foods I hated, especially the smell, which made me gag, and I had long since used up all the tricks of not eating it, like hiding pieces in my napkin and asking to be excused from the table to go to the bathroom. Now they knew better, and I was not excused. I had to eat all my food because there were plenty of starving people in India and China, which I hated for their starving, and because I should be thankful for what I got and I wasn't, even if it meant sitting alone at the kitchen table with a piece of cold liver long after everyone else had been excused, even if not eating it for supper meant I might get it again for breakfast, though I never did. No, it couldn't have been anything more serious than liver for supper or my mother would have said, "Just wait 'til your father gets home," and I would have waited in my room for the sound of his voice and footsteps moving down the hall in my direction. I would have waited to be taken to the basement, a condemned man in a cell. There my father would spank me with his belt, which only happened a couple times. The basement probably scared me more than the belt since I knew there were rats in the basement, which my mother had felt scurry across her feet when she went down there to wash clothes. We lived in an old apartment building, and no one ever visited the basement except to wash clothes or spank a boy who, as his father said, deserved whatever was coming to him. And long before I got to the basement stairs I cried about the rats and the drama of the belt slipping out of its loops—not the pain itself, which was never very much, and besides, when the pain came it meant that it was all over and I could stop crying. That was the way it worked.

It begins with me running from my father through the backyard of an old apartment building, running without thinking about where I'd go if I actually got away—like something I'd seen at the movies where someone chases someone else off the screen, like Tom and Jerry or Heckle and Jeckle at the Varsity Theater on Saturday afternoon. For there were as yet no TVs in the apartment house, only radios like the one in our kitchen, where I'd listen on Saturday mornings to *The Story Lady* or the Buster Brown Show, pretending I was a cowboy or a jungle boy or sometimes an orphan.

It begins with me running from a double-breasted brown suit and a boldly colored necktie, one of those ties I sometimes put on when we played car drivers in my bedroom. Bergy and I would be on kitchen chairs with pot lids from my mother's cupboard, which were the steering wheels we turned and turned and then made squealing noises, racing our chairs through the long afternoons. Our cars had running boards and special engines that would take us one hundred, two hundred, nine hundred miles an hour, in my father's ties, in my father's double-breasted suit coats that surrounded us like tents. Just about the only real driving was when my father took his upside-down-bathtub-shaped Ford out of the garage for a Sunday afternoon drive, or on those hot summer nights to follow a searchlight to its source and stop on the way home at the little store that sold double-dip ice cream cones for a nickel.

It begins with me running past the giant box elder tree in the backyard of the apartment building, the tree that came crashing down the night of the hundred-mile-an-hour wind, and in whose branches Bergy and I played, until the men with saws came and cut it up and hauled it away, with me running past the sandbox where Christopher—the son of Mother's friend, who'd come for a visit—and I packed sand into our ears because it looked so funny to do it, where my mother came out and said, "Just wait 'til your father gets home." And then my father did get home and drove us to the doctor's office where they squirted something into our ears and we cried, and the doctor said, "Boys will be boys," and my father laughed with him and never did take me to the basement with his belt, though I waited the rest of the day for him to do it.

It begins with me running toward the cars parked along the curb, where once I hit Diane, the daughter of another of my mother's friends, on the top of her head with a little stone, and Diane, who started bawling only when she reached the top of the back stairs, carried a chunk of tar as big as her hand to show her mother what I'd hit her with, and my mother said, "Just wait 'til your father gets home."

It begins with me running from a man I can't see or even hear behind me in a double-breasted brown suit with an orange-and-salmon-colored tie, who has just come home from work and who, just when I think I will run forever, catches me from behind, catches my Buster Brown oxford in his hand and trips me into a hard fall on the grass, where I sit amazed, looking up into his deep brown and blurry eyes, with grass stains on my knees, which my mother will soon be upset about, breathing in his dark tobacco smells as he asks me if I thought he couldn't run fast anymore, and I nod and wait for a blow that never comes, then feel his strong arms pulling me to my feet, leading me toward the flight of wooden stairs that runs up to the second floor balcony and then through our back door and into the kitchen, where my mother is cooking liver—which later, much later, I'd find out even she doesn't like—waiting and wondering where the two of us have run off to, and all the other things that she will never, ever know.

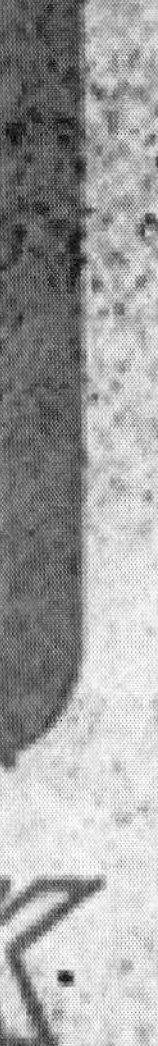

GOLD BOND STAMP
SAVERS BOOK

ONLY 1200 STAMPS
FILL THIS

S&H
GREEN STAMPS

QUICK
SAVER
BOOK
THE SPERRY AND HUTCHINSON COMPANY

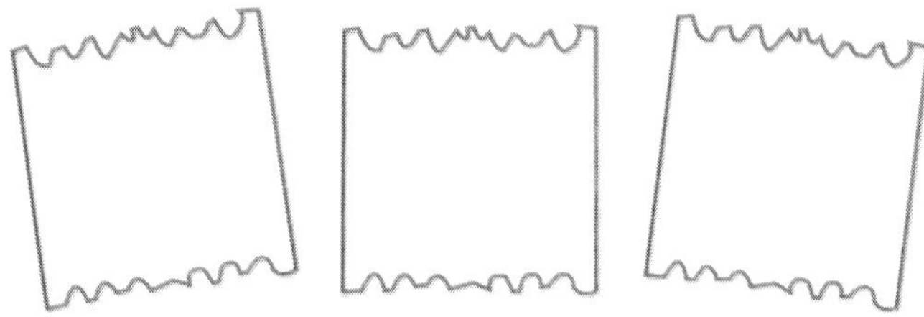

A Stitch in Time

Our apartment was in one of two small, two-story buildings next to each other in the shape of an L, with a driveway between them that led to a dirt oval in the backyard with clotheslines in the grassed-in middle and then a row of old garages and a woodpile. We lived in a second-floor corner apartment, right above the old man who was the building caretaker and his wife. There were three or four old women who lived by themselves in other apartments and a few married people, but the only other family with any children was Bergy's, who lived on the first floor of the other building. Mr. Mullen, the rent collector for the people who owned the place, lived in our building, too. His wife used to be an opera singer and sometimes sang so loudly in their apartment you could hear her right through the wall. My mother always told me to be extra good around Mr. Mullen or he might raise our rent. I wasn't sure if she was kidding, because she herself got all fluttery and smiley whenever he showed up at our back door.

Our first apartment was on the ground floor but was very small—I had to sleep on a rollaway behind a screen in the dining room. When I was six, my sister was born and we moved upstairs, which meant I also got my own room, even if it wasn't much bigger than a closet. My baby sister got a bigger room but had to share it whenever anyone came for a visit, like my grandmother from her small town in North Dakota, or my aunt Molly, my mother's older sister who had her own apartment across town but sometimes stayed over when it got too late to catch the bus home. My father traveled a lot because of his job, and there were times we wouldn't see him for a couple of weeks. That was when my mother said I'd have to be the man of the house, which I really didn't like, because I didn't want to be a grownup and we didn't live in a house.

My father used to say how sorry he was that he couldn't be around a lot more, and that he hoped that all the women in my life didn't get to be too much for me. I wasn't quite sure what he meant by that, unless it had something to do with all the advice I got from my mother or my aunt or grandmother or some of the old ladies I used to run errands for, which usually came in the form of sayings I had a hard time understanding, like "a stitch in time saves nine." I could *tell* time okay, but how could you *sew* it, and who were those nine who got saved? Then they'd tell me I shouldn't cut off my nose to spite my face, as if I would ever dream of doing such a painful thing.

They told me I couldn't have my cake and eat it too, but I knew I could, even if I only got cake on someone's birthday. What did they think I was going to do with my cake if not *eat* it?

"Curiosity killed the cat," they said, when I started asking questions. But we didn't have a cat. The apartment house didn't allow any animals. If I *could* have a pet, it would be a dog—which, after all, was man's best friend, and a boy would someday grow up to be a man.

I knew that little pitchers were supposed to have big ears, but my mother's pitcher in the cupboard didn't have ears at all. I'd heard, too, that I was getting too big for my britches, which probably had to do with my being fat, and that boys will be boys, which seemed pretty obvious.

Whenever I had questions, I'd ask Bergy, who was two years older, but he'd usually say he didn't really care and why should I?

"God moves in mysterious ways," my grandmother would tell me for just about everything I asked her.

"Just wait—it'll happen in good time," was what my mother liked to say. I had to wonder if that good time had a stitch in it, because it didn't often seem in any hurry to get around to me.

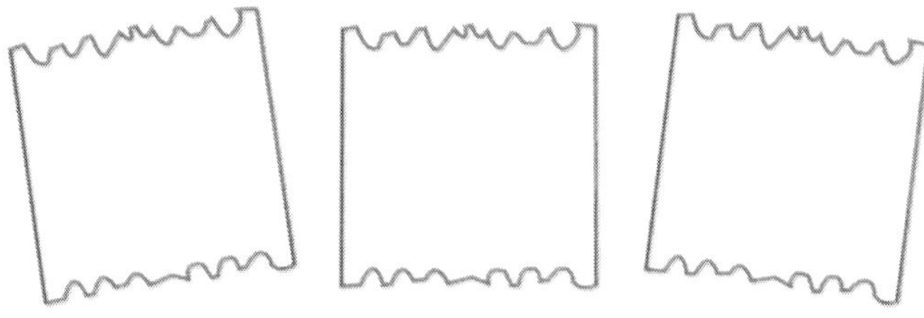

Mother's Helper

The part of the city where we lived was called Dinkytown, maybe because it contained a couple of blocks of stores where you could find just about everything you'd find in a much bigger place. Besides the Varsity Theater and Gray's drug store, there was Simm's hardware store and a butcher shop, a florist and a bakery, a barbershop, a dime store, a couple of restaurants, a little grocery store called the House of Hanson, Bridgeman's ice cream parlor, and two bookstores for the university, which was just beyond the overpass for the railroad tracks. A few blocks in the opposite direction were the busy, dangerous streets that led downtown and which both my mother and father had warned me about. But I never needed to go in that direction when the House of Hanson had such good penny candy and I could buy a small rose for a dime at the florist, wrapped up in green paper to take home and surprise my mother. All those stores were only about three blocks away from our apartment, along streets that weren't at all busy, though I still got told every day to stop and look both ways at the corners. And even if my father was away on a trip, I could always run to the store for whatever we needed, like half a pound of ground round at the butcher's or a loaf of bread from the Swedish bakery—usually with an extra nickel for a cookie for me to eat on the way home. And sometimes, on special occasions, I'd get to go pick up some chicken chow mein in one of those white cartons with the wire handles and then run most of the way home so it would still be warm when my mother spooned it onto our plates at the kitchen table. It was those times I didn't mind being the man of the house, heading off with my mother's carefully printed list and the money safe in the little coin purse in my pocket, and then walking home among all the grownups on the street, carrying my packages like they were just about the most important things I would ever carry in my life—and knowing that in some strange way, they probably were.

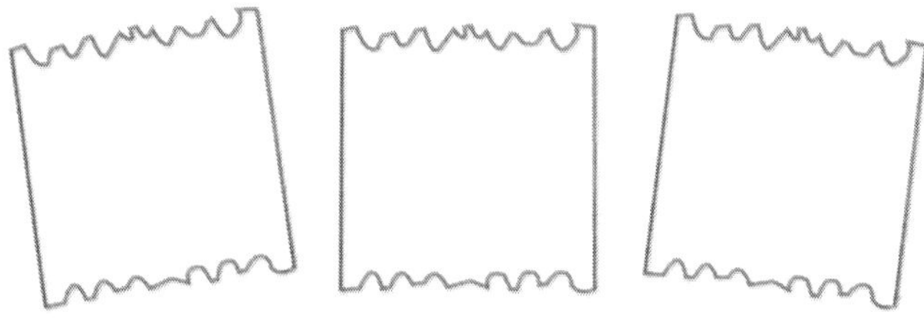

Just the Two of Us

Before my sister was born, my mother used to take me downtown on a big yellow streetcar. I really loved that clang and lurch and racket—I was sure when I grew up I'd drive a streetcar, admired by all as I turned the little crank on the glassed-in fare box people dropped their coins and tokens into, ringing the bell and peeling transfers from my pad. But it wasn't long before buses started replacing streetcars, even if it did take a long time for those tracks to get paved over. Buses weren't nearly as interesting, but it didn't really matter once we got downtown and visited our favorite stores and then had lunch at the Skyroom in the big department store called Dayton's, or at the Forum Cafeteria, where I got to carry my own tray and pick out my own food—within reason, my mother would remind me, meaning chocolate milk was okay but two desserts weren't.

Sometimes my mother shopped for things in the women's departments while I'd sit in a chair and watch the shoppers go by. Sometimes it was me who needed something, and we'd go places like the shoe store where you could look down into a screen and see the bones of your feet inside your shoes in this weird green light. Mostly we didn't buy anything except maybe some penny candy at Kresge's or Woolworth's, which were on opposite corners and were always crowded and smelled of popcorn and hot roasted peanuts and cashews.

But trips downtown weren't really about buying things or having lunch as much as walking around together through all those crowds of shoppers in all their different shapes and sizes and colors, or looking out the streetcar or bus windows at each new neighborhood we passed, wondering who lived in those houses and what they did, and then, on the way home, thinking about what we'd do the next time we went downtown together—back before my mother would have to stay home with my little sister and just about the time the streetcars began to disappear.

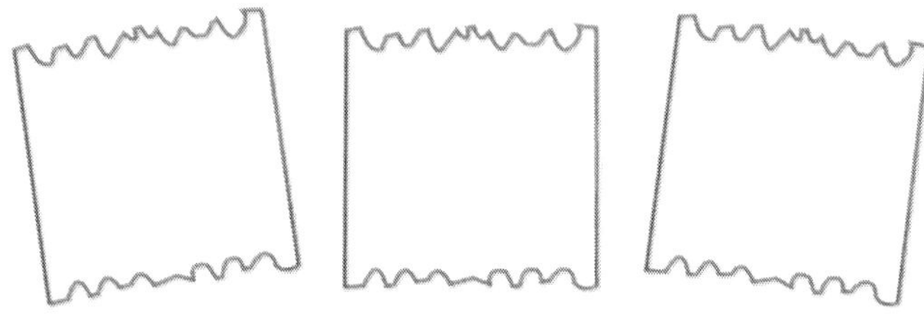

A Green Hill, Far Away

Every fall when the leaves were starting to get really pretty, we'd drive over to visit our cousins who lived in a town in Wisconsin, and sometimes my great aunt and uncle, who lived in a log cabin on top of a high hill. I knew it wasn't a very long drive, but it seemed a lot longer from the back seat, with not much to look at but leaves and every once in a while a small town or some grazing cows. There wasn't much to do at the farm either, except walk around and look at the cows from the next farm behind the fence, or the goats my Uncle Ed milked every day. Just to please him, I'd have to drink a little warm goat's milk and then, once or twice, I rode with him on his old black truck to take the cans of milk to town. As we went down the long grades of the highway, he'd turn the engine off and we'd coast. Sometimes the big trucks would come up behind us and blast their horns, but my uncle would just smile and talk about learning not to be in such a big hurry. I'd scrunch down in the seat so nobody could see me.

Our cousins lived in a small town, and when we'd spend the night at their house, I'd have to sleep on the sofa, where my mother would line up dining room chairs so I wouldn't roll off. The best thing about those trips was how safe and warm I'd feel there in my little nest, as she called it, which I'd imagine was high on top of one of those green hills, high above the cows and goats and highways, as I'd listen to the sounds of grown-up voices talking and laughing in the distance, growing fainter and fainter, farther and farther away.

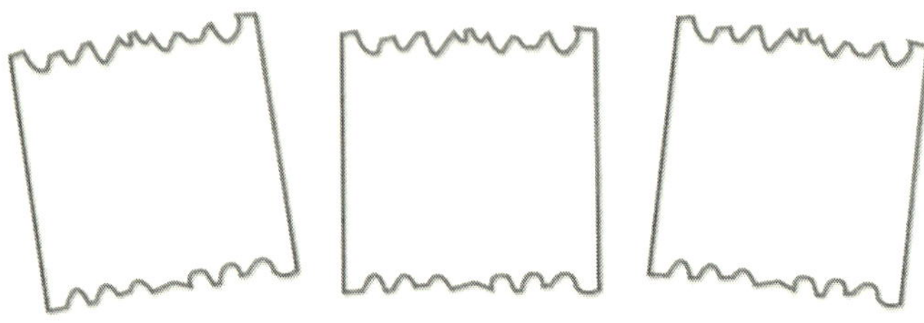

How I Flunked Knot Tying

The first thing I remember about starting school at Marcy Elementary was one day when our kindergarten teacher decided that her pupils should at least know how to tie a simple knot. "It isn't very hard at all," she said, passing out thick green school pencils to us all, along with pieces of string. "Watch carefully now," she told us, demonstrating the proper technique, and before long most of kids had it down pat. Except for me, because I was so fascinated by the new green pencil that I hadn't listened to the teacher's instructions, which probably wasn't the first time that had happened. Maybe it had been a bad day for her, or maybe I just deserved it. What she needed was to make an example of me by holding up my new green pencil just beyond my grasp, and my limp, knotless string. "This will never do," she clucked, and everybody was gathered around us laughing, and this kid I already hated from Sunday school suddenly handed her his pencil with a perfect two inch row of knots topped off by a bow—the kind my mother tied my shoes with, the kind that was still a complete mystery to most of us. He just handed it to the teacher with a grin and didn't say anything at all.

The next day, which was Saturday, I spent the entire morning by the radio tying knots—rows and rows of them, on every piece of string and pencil I could find. Someday they were going to tear that old school down and I would be there to watch, wearing beautiful bows.

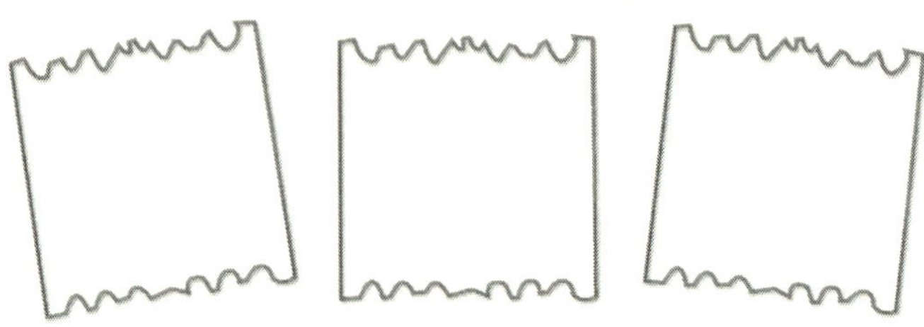

Primer Lesson

Some nights my mother would read to me from *A Child's Garden of Verses*, a strange world where children talked like grownups and had nannies and counterpanes and there were a lot of other things I'd never heard of. But I was learning to read, too, from the Dick and Jane books at school, another place that sometimes bewildered me—where everyone always smiled and was unbelievably polite, where there never seemed to be any kind of trouble at all. How I marveled at Dick and Jane's perfect house and parents, and especially at their little dog Spot, who could get everyone excited just by jumping up. "Look!" they'd all shout, "See Spot run!" as if that were some sort of miracle.

I had to face it—as much as I liked their dog, Dick and Jane weren't the kind of kids I'd want for friends, any more than the ones who had nannies and didn't get to go outside by themselves. My mother never wore necklaces and high heels around the apartment, either, and Dick and Jane's father never sat in the kitchen in his undershirt. It was Dick and Jane's father I wondered about the most. I finally decided he'd probably give just about anything to get away somewhere for a smoke and a beer. "Look, look!" they all would shout, "See Father run!"

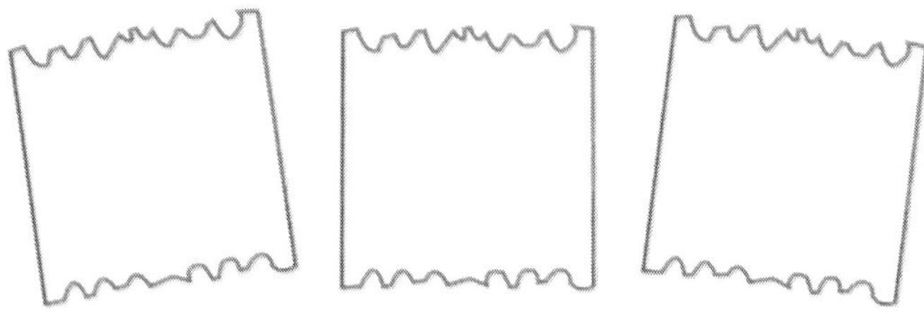

Art Education

In second grade, we had to learn handwriting and try to make our letters just like the ones on those cards above the blackboard, which I had a hard time doing. Not many of the girls seemed to have trouble with penmanship, and not with drawing and coloring, either, which were something I really wanted to be good at. In third grade, when our teacher put our drawings up on the classroom bulletin boards, none of the girls ever said anything about mine, especially not my horses, which looked more like cows. Then I got the idea to use a book to copy my drawing from, maybe because I found the perfect picture of a cowboy on a horse, twirling a lariat. I practiced drawing it in pencil and then used my outline one day at school to make the best crayon drawing I'd ever done—just as good as the drawings of some of the girls, who even said for the first time that they liked my picture, that it was good enough to go on the bulletin board outside our room, where everyone in the school could see it.

When it came time to bring our pictures home to show our parents, my mother taped mine to the refrigerator, where it stayed for a long time—always reminding me of how I'd cheated, till I couldn't bear to look at it any more and took it down and tore it up. It was quite a while before my mother even realized it was gone. One of her friends had stopped by and asked about me, so my mother thought she'd show her my picture. When my mother asked me what had happened to it I said I didn't know, maybe my little sister had taken it. One thing I was sure about—even if my picture did impress some of the girls, I promised myself I was never going to do anything like that again, though I also had the feeling that when girls were involved, that kind of promise might not matter very much.

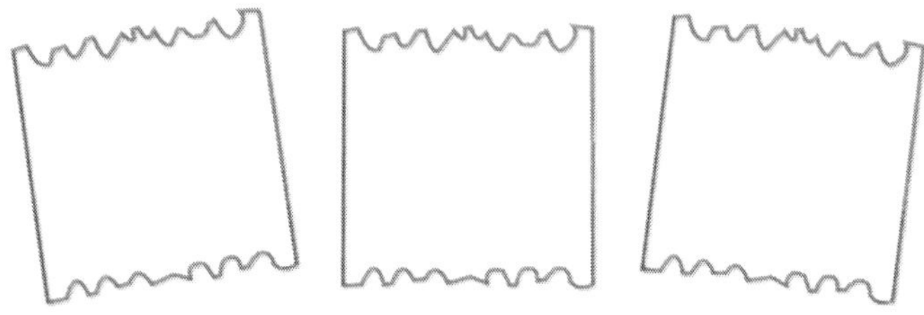

Underground

The door to our basement opened on a laundry room with wringer washers for all the apartments, wooden racks for drying clothes, and shelves lined with Tide and Oxydol and bottles of blueing. But there were other rooms, too, a dusty maze of rooms with an open pit in one of them, which my mother constantly warned me about. She also said that sometimes when she went to hang up wash she could hear rats or even feel them scurrying across her feet. I never saw any rats, but I never went very far into the labyrinth either, even if I imagined there might be something pretty interesting in there.

The basement of the apartment house next door was a lot better—the walls were whitewashed and there was a secret place under the stairs where Bergy and I would light candles and look at his horror comics like *Tales from the Crypt*. Down the block, my friend Denny's father hung up dead deer in his basement, and Robert's house across the street had a basement room full of books and a big table, where his sister, who went to the university, used to draw insects—dark, strange drawings of beetles with huge pincers and worm-like things with dozens of feet. Robert said his sister had cancer and spent most of her time in the hospital now. I couldn't help wondering if there was some connection to that creepy room.

The basement at school seemed mostly corridors with dim lights and the sound of humming machinery. Once in a while we all had to go down there for A-bomb drills and sit on the concrete floor against the wall with our heads between our knees. Even with our teachers in charge, it always felt like something terrible was about to happen—something that didn't have anything to do with A-bombs.

Whenever I had nightmares about dark places underground, they were of that school basement and of all the kids lining up in the corridors with startled looks on their faces. If I had a choice, I'd take my chances with scary beetles, skinned deer, rats, even open pits—not those cold-tiled walls with the giant machines humming, where nobody dared to say a word.

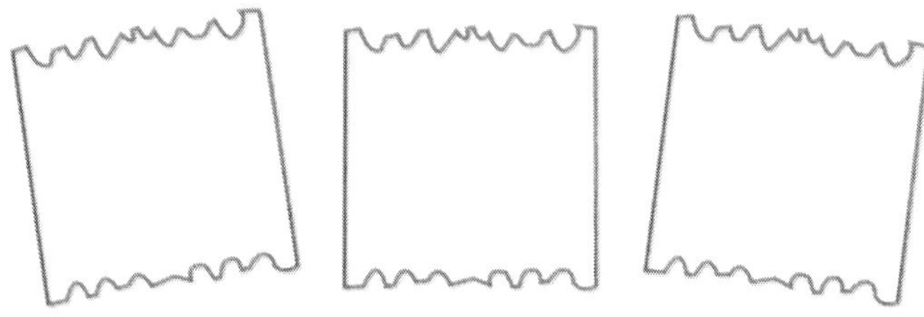

Natural History

Whenever we found a dead sparrow in the grass, we'd dig a hole and give it a proper burial, as Bergy called it, right down to singing "Jesus Loves Me" and making a cross to mark the grave with out of Popsicle sticks. One day we found a bird we hadn't come across before, mostly red, with black wings, and Bergy got the idea we should put it in his wagon and take it over to the Natural History Museum at the university. It might be some kind of rare species and maybe even worth some money.

I got so excited at the thought of that, I forgot to tell my mother—or, rather, ask her permission—and I didn't remember till we were crossing University Avenue, the busiest street around, which we'd never done before. But it was too late to turn back, and when we brought the bird up the big front steps the man at the door smiled and took us down a long hallway past some offices, to a large room where three or four people were working on different kinds of dead birds, cutting them open and mounting them in all kinds of ways. The man slid out drawers with whole trays full of dead birds to show us, and one of them had several just like the one we had found, which the man said was a scarlet tanager and that even if it wasn't worth any money, it would be a nice addition to their collection.

I'd been to that museum to see all the stuffed animals with my parents, but I'd never really thought about how those animals got there in the first place, which made me feel creepier than I'd ever felt before. But not Bergy, who said on the way home that he'd already decided he was going to be some kind of scientist and that getting to work on dead birds and animals would be the kind of thing that scientists had to learn how to do.

When we got home I wanted to tell my mother just what we'd done and seen but that would also mean she'd find out I'd gone all that way without her permission and I'd really be in trouble. There were so many questions I wanted to ask her, but I just couldn't.

After that, Bergy and I didn't have funerals for birds anymore, though sometimes I'd think about those big rooms where they were cutting open dead things. If Bergy was sure he was going to be a scientist when he grew up, then I was just as sure I wasn't.

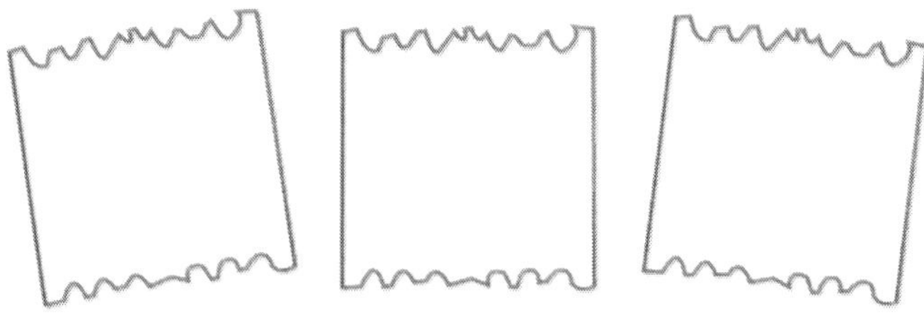

Wash Day

Sometimes I'd help my mother lug the wicker basket full of wet clothes up the steps from the basement laundry room, the smell of soap and blueing rising from her dress. "I hope it's good drying weather," she'd say, and I'd hand her the clothespins one by one, the little stiff-legged creatures who sometimes were my toys on days it rained, or the other kind, with springs, which Bergy and I would make into shooters for wooden matches he'd sneak from his mother. "I wonder what's been happening to all my clothespins," my mother would say with a frown. But she also said how nice it was to have a little company, especially when the clothes were dry, smelling of sun and trees, and it was time to take the loaded basket up the stairs to the kitchen, where I could help her sprinkle them before she ironed. I loved to watch the wrinkles disappear beneath the iron as she worked away, the two of us in the kitchen, or out on the back porch steps, watching the billowing sheets on the clotheslines, or if there were any dark clouds moving in, trying to decide the right time to take down the wash before it started to rain. Sometimes we'd get caught in a shower, but what really mattered was my mother saying again how she couldn't have done the job without me.

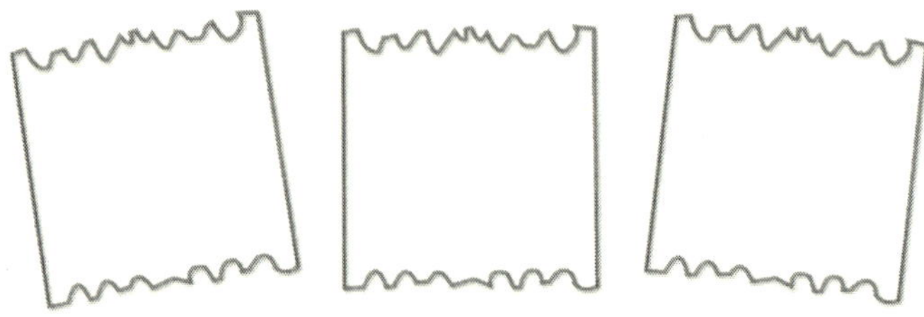

Mixed Blessings

Aunt Molly was my mother's older sister and my favorite relative because she always gave me the best presents, like the life-sized Gene Autry six-shooter cap pistol and a pair of cowboy boots, which I wanted more than anything in the world and knew I'd never get from my parents. My father always seemed a little angry with her for spoiling me, but I also knew that he didn't like her very much because she usually drank too many highballs and got my mother to join her, especially when Aunt Molly came over when my father was away on a trip. Whenever I found ginger ale in the refrigerator and no one was sick, I knew that Aunt Molly would be coming over, because that's what she used to make her highballs, though I also heard her say that in her apartment she just kept the whiskey bottle in the Fridge so she wouldn't have to fool with ginger ale or even ice cubes.

Aunt Molly always brought some Coca Cola, too, which is what she drank at the rest home where she was a nurse, and plenty of cigarettes. Once, when we all were visiting some relatives and she and I had to share a room, I hardly slept all night because she was smoking in bed and I was terrified she'd burn us all up. I'd watch the red glow of her cigarette from my bed across the room, and just when she'd finally put it out and I'd think it was safe to go to sleep, she'd light up again.

Besides giving me presents and scaring me, my aunt usually defended me to my father, telling him he was just too hard on me. But it seemed okay for her to be hard on me, like the night she and my mother were up late drinking highballs in the kitchen right next to my bedroom and she woke me up with her screaming about what a spoiled, lazy lunk I was and how I'd probably never amount to anything. After that, I was never as happy to see her, no matter what she brought me, though I was always careful to do everything she told me, and I never once mentioned how those cowboy boots pinched my toes so badly I couldn't even wear them outside.

Sam Hill, Jack Robinson, and Me

"Where in the Sam Hill have you been?" my father would yell at me when I came in late. I didn't know who this Sam Hill was, but he always made my father angry. I just hated it when Sam Hill was around with his beady little face, always waiting to make trouble when my father got home. And that's not to mention his friend Jack Robinson. My father would say he was going to paddle my butt as quick as Jack Robinson, or that if I knew what was good for me I'd finish my vegetables quick as Jack Robinson. It seemed sometimes that the apartment wasn't big enough for the three of us any more. A couple of us were going to have to go—and most days, I got the feeling that one of them was going to be me.

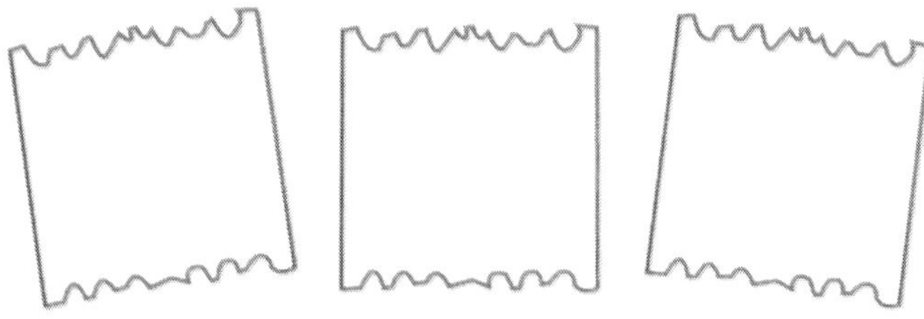

Religious Education

At the opposite end of the block from our apartment house was a big Lutheran church, the one my parents went to sometimes, where I had to go to Sunday school, and where every so often there were smorgasboard dinners in the basement. Not far away was a big Catholic church, which was mainly a mystery to Bergy and me. What we did know was that the Catholic kids weren't afraid to swear, and they could tell some pretty strange stories, like going to confession. Some of the old women who lived in the apartments went to the Catholic church every day—and that more than anything else made me glad I wasn't a Catholic.

My mother sometimes told stories about the small town she'd grown up in, which was also where my grandparents still lived and where I'd get sent to visit every summer. In that town, everyone went either to the Catholic church or the Lutheran church, and my mother told me that when she was my age she sometimes got into trouble for going to mass with her Catholic friends.

Sonny Sadler's family lived down by the railroad tracks in that town, and he told me once that only Catholics could get into heaven. Sonny was only 12, but he already smoked and said he drank whiskey too, so I really had to wonder how he figured he was going anywhere close to heaven. When I asked her, my mother said we'd all go to the same place, Catholics or Lutherans or whatever, but when I asked her about people in far away places who never even heard of Jesus, all she said was that God moved in mysterious ways.

If church was about going to such a happy place as heaven, it was always a huge mystery to me why it had to be so boring. Sometimes when my father was home we'd all have to go to the Sunday service. The first part wasn't so bad, especially with the hymn singing, but by the time the minister got to his sermon I was really bored—which got worse when it sounded like he was coming to the end and he'd keep going on and on. To keep from falling asleep, I'd try to count all the panes in all the stained glass windows I could see, and sometimes I'd look up at all the dark beams in that high church ceiling and pretend I was up there on a trapeze, doing death-defying swings high above the heads of the congregation, and then they'd look up at me in amazement, not at the preacher in his pulpit.

Once, when my father was away on a trip and my mother was home in bed with a headache, I decided to stick around for church after Sunday school to make her happy. I sat up towards the front, where my family usually sat so my father could hear what was being said, and after the opening part of the service and the first hymn, and before the preacher could start his sermon, I walked back up that long aisle and out the church doors. The people I walked by seemed pretty surprised, and when I got home and told my mother that I'd gone to the first part of church all by myself to make her feel better, she cried and hugged me and told me how much she loved me and never to do that again.

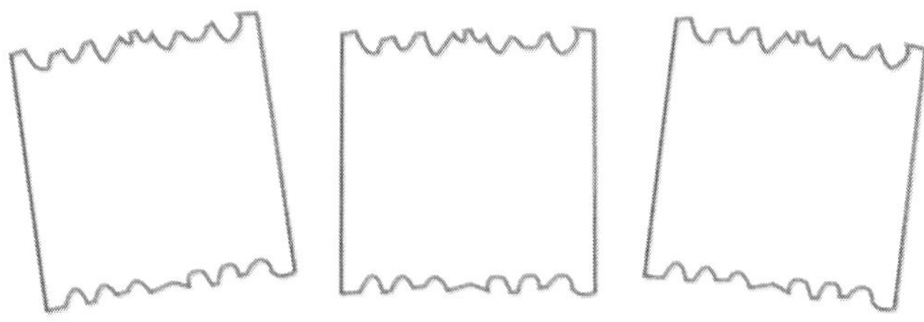

Using My Head

I used to be curious about where my father worked, until one Saturday morning when he took me with him to get something from his office in the old Federal Building on Washington Avenue downtown. It was a street where the people on crutches and the raggedy men who drank from paper bags both fascinated and frightened me, as did the basement of that building with its rickety old freight elevator. I couldn't help thinking about terrible things like rats in that dark basement where he searched through cardboard files and boxes, and I couldn't help but imagine being trapped down there without the hope of ever seeing daylight again, not even the daylight on skid row, which is what my mother called the neighborhood where he parked the car.

"I won't feed those meters," my father would say, so we'd drive around and around the blocks of staring, staggering men, trying to find a place to park that didn't have a meter. Once, my father stopped in an alley behind a cafe and when we were getting out of the car, a man with a grimy apron and a little paper hat came out of a door and asked us for a quarter to park there, and my father made me get back in the car and drive around with him some more. Even though it was more than my whole weekly allowance, I wished I had a quarter to give to that man in the paper hat, to hide the burning red I felt in my face.

I always ended up afraid I was going to let my father down by not having a very good time on those days we were together, maybe because I knew my father just wanted to spend time with me since he had to be gone so much. "Look for a parking place," my father would say. "Use your head." I stared so hard I hurt my eyes, but all the places I found were in front of fireplugs or somewhere else that parking wasn't allowed. In all that driving around I never found a place, I never used my head.

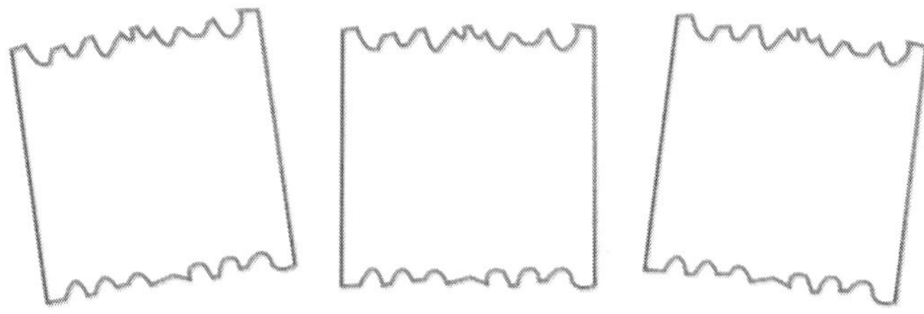

Tracks

Sometimes my father took me to the Milwaukee Road station downtown, where we'd watch the people getting on the shiny passenger trains and I'd try to imagine where they were going. Then we'd wave like crazy as the trains pulled away. I really loved to see trains, no matter where we were.

I must have been only four or five years old when I went on my first train trip. My grandmother took me on the Empire Builder to her small town in North Dakota and what I liked the best was looking out the window when we went through towns, especially as we passed the red semaphore lights and clanging bells.

Sometimes lying in bed at night I'd hear a train whistle far away and it always sounded so lonely. But then I'd remember that first trip all over again, watching myself trying to see past my reflection in the glass, feeling safe and loved, and thinking of all the others at either end of the trip. What a disappointment I was going to be to some of them, what a joy to others, but for that moment what I knew best was that from inside the train that whistle didn't sound lonely at all.

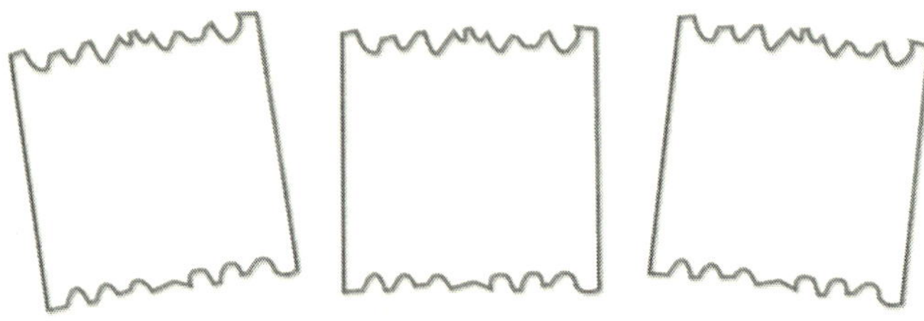

The Mortality Rate

One of the kids in my class had a baby brother with some kind of rare disease that made his head almost the same size as his body. Jerry kept telling me that what his brother had wasn't catching but I still wouldn't even have a glass of Kool Aid at Jerry's house. I couldn't help staring at the baby in his highchair, his head flopping and his eyes rolling. Jerry said that his brother would probably die before long and he couldn't wait till they moved his brother to the hospital so Jerry could have his room to himself again.

Jerry really shocked me when he said that, but my Aunt Molly, who was a nurse, talked the same way about some of the old people she took care of— that they should just get it all over with and quit being a burden on everyone else. She'd spent most of her life around sick old people and she was getting damned tired of it.

Sometimes she'd talk about the polio hospital which our city was famous for—sometimes we'd go right by it on the bus and I always held my breath till we were safely past. There was a lot about polio in the newspapers and on the radio, especially in the summer, when some of the swimming pools got closed and I usually got sent to spend some time with my grandparents in their small town in North Dakota. I didn't know anybody who'd gotten polio, though Robert, who lived in the house across the street, talked a lot about his sister in the hospital with cancer.

Those were the kind of creepy things we liked to talk about, sometimes on the street corner in front of the apartment buildings. And then we'd get around to talking about ourselves, too. Bergy had broken his arm and said he still had a pin in it, and Robert had a long scar on his leg where he said he'd gotten caught on a barbed wire fence at his uncle's farm. The only scar I had was covered up by hair, but I could still tell the story about the time my friend Stevie accidentally hit me in the head with a golf club when we went with our fathers to the golf course in my grandparents' town. I could tell what it felt like to get knocked out and about how all the blood ruined my shirt. What I never could say was how upset my father looked when he came driving in his car right across the golf course to take me to the clinic, where I got five stitches. Even if he never said anything about it except that I'd had a really close call, I wished I could have explained the look on his face to Bergy and the others—out there on our street corner bragging about wounds, even if we somehow knew that it didn't really count.

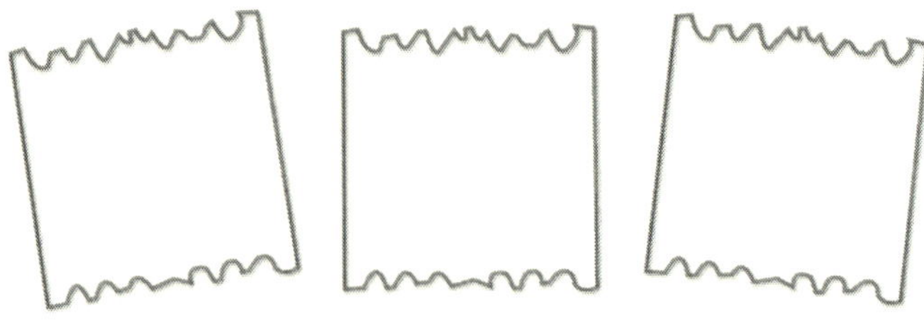

How It Was Going

There were times my mother didn't get out of bed for most of the day and I'd have to watch my little sister. Once in a while Aunt Molly came by after work and made supper for us—she said my mother had migraines and had to take strong medicine for them, all of which I didn't really understand, except that sometimes when she got them she scared me with the way she acted, all groggy and confused, even knocking dishes off the table or forgetting to turn off water in the tub. When I tried to tell her how upset she was making me I couldn't get her to understand, not even the next day when she was acting normal again. My aunt just said that I should be thankful to have such a good mother who did so much for me and did I ever stop to think it might be me who was giving her those migraines in the first place? Maybe someday I'd have a kid of my own who gave me migraines, which would serve me right.

I never did talk to my father about those migraines, because if what my aunt said about me causing them was true, I'd just be getting myself in trouble. So, whenever he asked me how things had been going at home when he was on the road, I'd just say pretty good, and then he'd smile and ask me again if I knew how much everybody was counting on me, and I'd say yes, I guessed I did, and no, I wouldn't forget it, not ever.

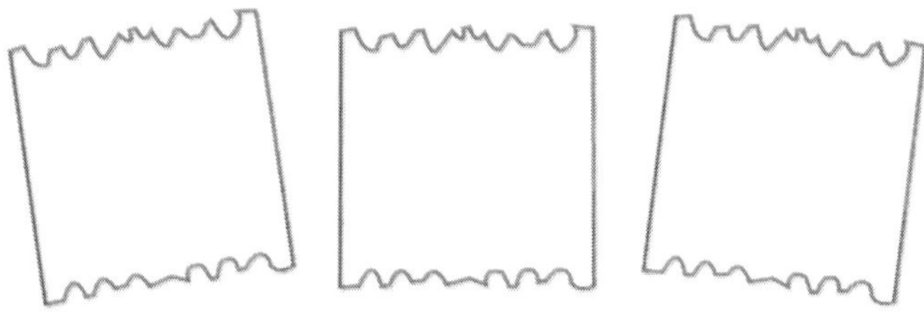

Blood Brothers

Bergy and I saw it in the Saturday matinee at the Varsity Theater, so of course we had to try it ourselves. These two guys—a cowboy and an Indian—took knives and cut their wrists and then pressed their two wrists together so they could be "blood brothers." It didn't seem to hurt them. They just acted strong and stared into each other's eyes. It looked pretty neat.

When we got back home we went out to Bergy's garage to do the ceremony. Bergy got real excited, like I'd never seen him act before. He knew that blood was really blue when it was inside your body, but the instant it touched the air it turned red. He kept looking at the vein on the inside of his wrist like this might be the chance to prove something to me.

But our mothers wouldn't let us play with knives, and the old jacknife we found in the vacant lot was so rusty we couldn't even get it open. I did have this safety pin where a button was missing on my shirt, so I thought that might work just as well. After all, it could still draw some blood, couldn't it? That got Bergy mad at me. He said I was a sissy so I pushed him down and sat on his chest till he said I was his best friend, and we finally agreed to try it with the pin. But he'd get to do the sticking for both of us—in our fingers, not our wrists—and we couldn't flinch.

It really hurt, too, but I only jumped a little bit and Bergy said it was probably okay. But when he saw the blood coming out of the end of my finger he got kind of funny in the face and said that he really had to go home for supper or he'd get a licking for sure. I guess I could have just stood there with blood dripping out of my finger, but I couldn't let Bergy get away with that, so I pushed him down again and took the pin away from him and stuck his finger hard and then pushed our two fingers together so we'd be blood brothers just like in the movie. Bergy was crying and called me a fat shit and said we'd probably get an infection in our fingers and have to got to the doctor and maybe even have our fingers cut off.

I kept away from Bergy for a long time after that, and even if my finger didn't get infected after all, I started wondering what if some of Bergy's blood really got inside of me? It made me nervous to think I might start to act just like Bergy, and even though we never even talked about being blood brothers again, I had to wonder if Bergy ever wondered if he was going to start acting just like me.

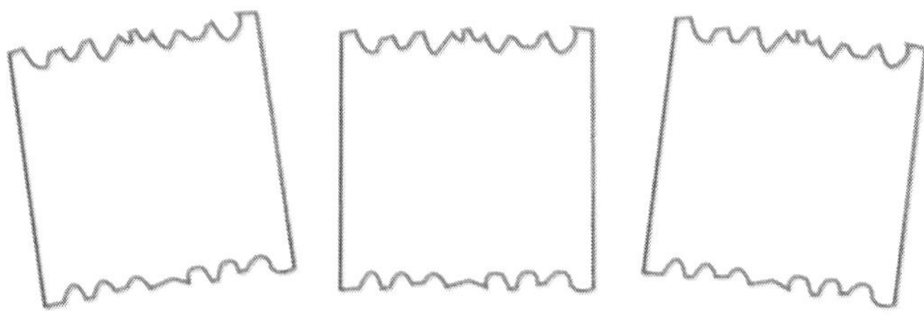

Original Sin

Our teacher told us if we caused trouble at school it might get put on our permanent record, which made me think of some huge old dusty book and the kind of ink that would never come off. I also tried to imagine what might be written about me in that book—and from how far back.

All the classroom walls in Marcy Elementary seemed to have big framed pictures of famous people, like Abraham Lincoln, who probably didn't have anything bad in his permanent record—no black marks against him, as my mother put it. She also said she couldn't figure out why I disliked going to school so much, especially since she'd been a grade school teacher herself for a few years, back before she and my father got married. I couldn't imagine my mother being the kind of teacher who'd make you stand up next to your desk and get yelled at when you'd done something wrong. And I didn't know how to tell her that whenever I had to stand up next to my desk, all I could think about was whether or not my teacher would be writing something down in my permanent record—and how it would keep following me, no matter how old I got, wherever I went.

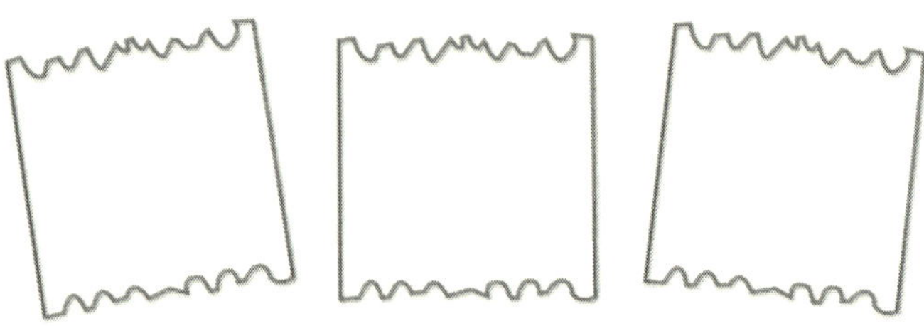

Sociology

Bergy said his father was a Chevy man, which meant a Chevy was the only kind of car he'd ever own. When I asked my father about that, he said he'd owned a Chevy once, too, but then a Dodge and two Fords because those were what he'd gotten the best deals on. What was I to do about that kind of indifference, anyway? Without an argument, Bergy decided we were Ford people, pure and simple. At least we were second best.

"Let's talk about Republicans and Democrats," Bergy said, but I couldn't bear the thought of what I'd probably find out—even if I wasn't sure what those words meant. At least we weren't Nash people or Studebaker people. Bergy decided it wasn't so bad being Ford people as long as there was *somebody* to make fun of. I had to admit my relief. I had to hand it to him for *that*.

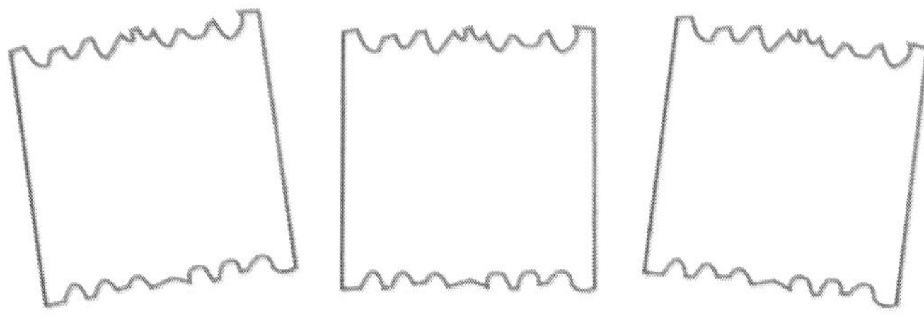

Not-So-Good Friday

My mother said we should give up something we loved for Lent, which in my case would have to be candy. It wouldn't be so bad, she said, when we considered the Catholics, who had to give up meat every Friday, though she herself could eat fish six days a week if she had to, and I had to be thankful that was something that never happened. She could make giving up sweets sound pretty good, not to mention improving my waistline.

Even if my mother didn't allow anything good to eat during Lent, I could usually find a nickel somewhere for candy at the little store across from school. You're killing Our Lord all over again, my mother would say when she'd find those wrappers I couldn't seem to hide. It wasn't a matter of going to hell, which I knew was a lot worse. But I also knew that if God was really Love, then how could He demand I give up what I wanted most?

When I got up on Good Friday, the apartment was dark and I could hear hymns playing on the radio. I could tell my mother had been crying, too, so I mostly stayed in my room, thinking about Jesus up there on His cross like she'd asked me to do, thinking about my father, who couldn't make it home from the road, but thinking more about stuffing myself with Easter candy in just days, and sometimes even wondering why I had to do it.

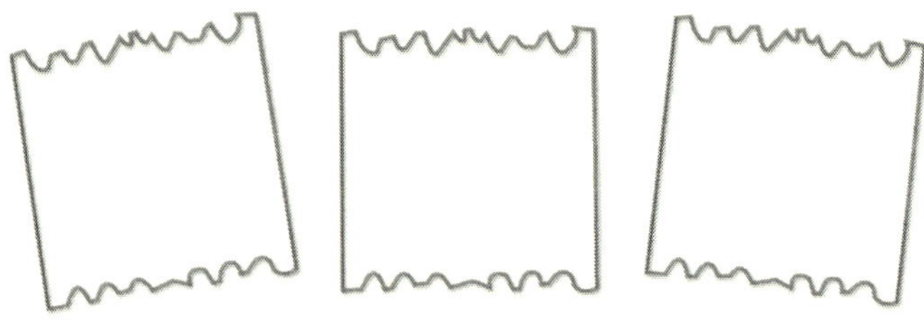

A Short History of the War

The summer I was ten, we discovered "Freedom's War" bubblegum cards. The one I remember best was called *Point Blank Range* and pictured this American soldier in Korea emptying his .45 into a bunch of red Chinese soldiers about to overrun his howitzer position. Some of the cards had pictures of different kinds of guns or planes or tanks, with descriptions on the back of the card, but a lot of them had drawings of battle scenes with stories of places like Heartbreak Ridge, which is a name we'd repeat to each other when we went on patrol in the vacant lot across from the Catholic church, which was filled with tall weeds. Bergy had a plastic .45 and his father's old steel helmet, so of course he got to be the patrol leader. Robert, from the house on the corner across the street, sometimes played guns with us and brought along his brother's bb-gun, but since the only gun I had was a cowboy cap pistol, I had to carry a baseball bat and pretend it was a bazooka.

That was the summer this kid named Bobby, who'd been in my room at school, died when he fell through the skylight of some church while he was up on the roof hunting pigeons with his bow and arrow, about the same time one of my mother's cousin's kids got taken to the hospital with polio. It was the summer, too, when we learned how to pour gasoline on grasshoppers and light them on fire on the dirt floor of Bergy's father's garage. There were millions of grasshoppers in the Catholic's weed field and we'd found some gasoline in a rusty old can someone had left by the woodpile. It wasn't hard to find matches lying around by our fathers' ashtrays or on the shelves above our mothers' gas stoves. "Take that, you dirty Commies," we'd scream as those hoppers shriveled and popped in the flames. "Point Blank Range!"

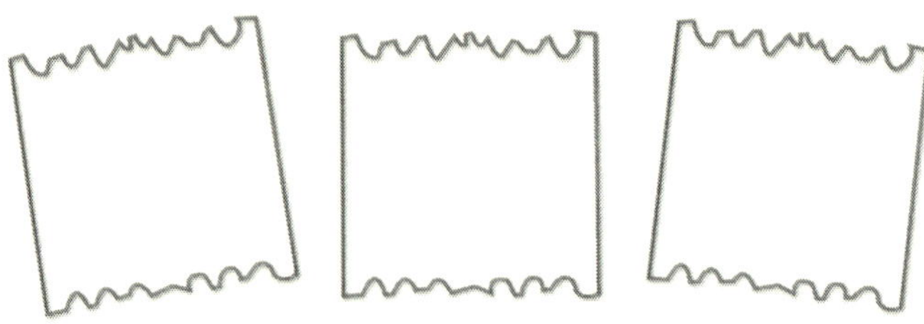

Lessons

"Heave it," Bergy cried. "Chuck it, fling it." That's what we did most days—any kind of ball or rock, crabapples, marbles, sticks, whatever we could find in the apartment house garbage out back. "Tell me why you boys are always throwing things," my mother said, and I knew the lecture was coming, the one about learning my lesson, the one about putting someone's eye out. I never did, though there were times when I came close—the kid whose glasses I cracked with pebbles in the schoolyard, the daughter of my mother's friend I beaned with a little rock, and even Bergy, the day I laid him out with a softball. "Some throw," Bergy said, and didn't come out to play with me for a couple of days. "Wait till your father gets home," my mother said when she put down the phone. So I waited out in front and bounced a golf ball off the steps and wall until I messed up, of course, and broke a basement window. Maybe it was then I learned for the first time how hopeless I could be. Or maybe it was just the summer afternoon, the thwack of the ball against the bricks, the empty streets and sidewalks, without a soul in sight.

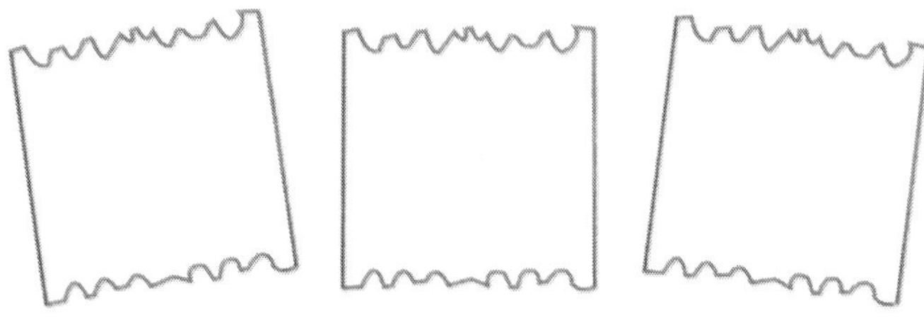

Theology

Bergy said that going to school on Sunday was about the dumbest thing he'd ever heard of—didn't I get enough school during the week? I tried to show him the presents they gave me, like the picture of Jesus steering the ship. "Isn't He supposed to walk on water?" Bergy said. "What's he need a ship for, anyway?" I had to wonder about that, and about the teacher's other stories, too, like all those plagues, or the time God turned the foolish lady into salt. This Sunday stuff was risky business, but Bergy didn't seem to care a bit. His parents didn't even go to church.

There he'd sit on Sunday mornings, out on the front porch with the funny papers, watching me trudge off to Bible class. "Ask them to give you some of their wine," he'd yell, and when I finally did, the teacher said I was in big trouble. I prayed to Jesus to get me out of that one, but He never did—sailing off into the clouds with me alone in the corner, and in my foolish mouth the unmistakable taste of salt.

The Silver Screen

Roy Rogers was King of the Cowboys, Gene Autry the Prince of the Plains. " A king is better than a prince," Bergy said. "Everyone knows you just like Gene Autry because he's fat, like you." That's the way it went each Saturday— ten cartoons and a cowboy movie at the Varsity matinee. The only times we didn't argue were when they'd bring in Tim Holt or Lash LaRue or some other commoner. But there was war, too, and Abbott and Costello. They knew what would keep us cheering through the Previews, get us to spend our allowances on Root Beer Barrels and soda pop—down in the fourth row from the front, where everything stuck to the floor.

And then we'd go home to act out every scene, and dream ourselves away from parents, rules, and chores. " I can't wait to grow up," Bergy said. I wasn't sure what he meant by that, except that he was older and smarter, as he kept reminding me. Maybe he *should* be King of the Cowboys, galloping off ahead of me each Saturday—all those winding trails and darkening hills.

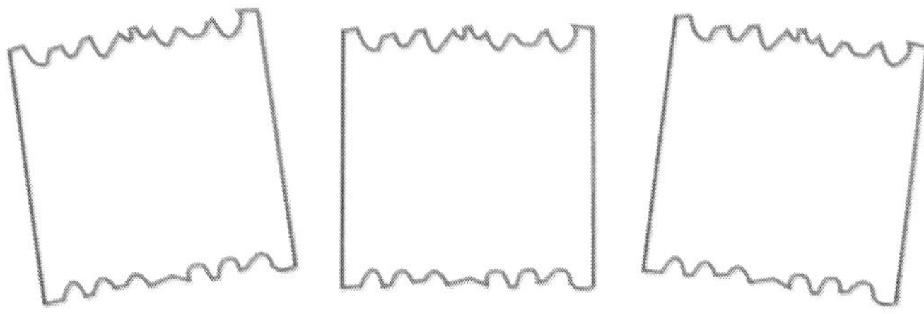

Trophies

My father had a friend from work who lived on a little lake and kept inviting him to come out, so one Saturday as a complete surprise, my father decided to take me fishing at his friend's place. We sat in a boat for a long time, drowning worms, as my father's friend said, until I finally caught a little sunfish, which the men wanted to put back in the lake. But I had to bring it home to show my mother, who said she was really proud, and then Bergy, who said it was pretty good—for me. That same day, he and his father had been hiking by the Mississippi and found a big snapping turtle, which was out on Bergy's back porch in a bucket. A bunch of neighborhood kids came over to see it and we all stood around for a long time trying to get it to eat something, trying to get it to snap at sticks. "Watch your stupid fingers," Bergy kept saying, waving us back with his mother's yardstick. The next morning I found my sunfish in the garbage, wrapped up in the Sunday comics and beginning to stink.

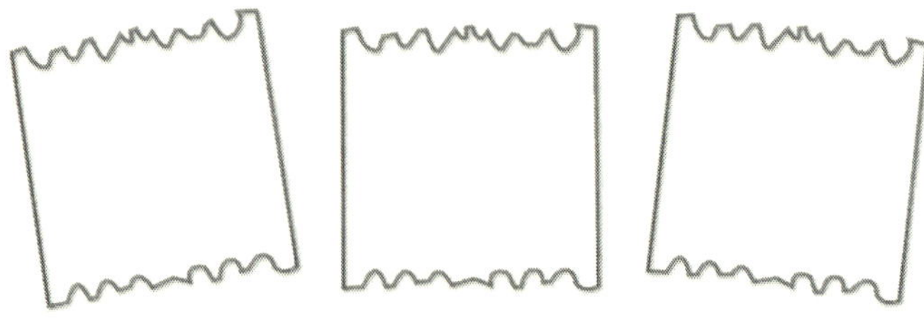

Center of Attention

My father said that most of the trouble I got into was because I was afraid of missing out on something. Maybe that was why I never wanted to go to bed and had such a hard time getting to sleep. When I asked Bergy, he said, sure, I liked to butt into where it was none of my beeswax, which reminded me of the time I got stung by a wasp when I was trying to see what was under some old boards in the woodpile.

My mother kept telling me not to worry about what other people did or thought—which only seemed to work if I didn't really care about those people, like the old ladies in our apartment buildings, who were always peeking out their windows to see what was going on.

At school, sometimes, I'd really get embarrassed if the teacher called on me, though I also liked it too, especially when I knew the answer. That was the way I felt about being one of the few boys in the highest reading group, too, or getting good things written on my report cards.

Everyone probably knew the biggest problem I had in school—and probably at home, too—was daydreaming. Maybe that was why I sometimes felt that everybody else in class knew something important, something I was supposed to know but didn't. And that's when I was sure that the teacher was going to call on me and that soon everybody would be whispering about me, like grownups sometimes whispered, and that's when I wanted more than anything in the world to know what they were saying. How could they blame me for wondering what they didn't want me to know?

Killing Time

It was on the bridge over the railroad tracks where we'd walk sometimes on our way to look for empty Coke bottles by the university—where, if we were lucky, we could stand in the flood of smoke and steam from those old engines chuffing underneath us. Just like the fog in monster movies, Bergy would say. Leave it to Bergy to come up with a good adventure for free, even if we'd have to wait a long time to find it.

Afterwards, our mothers would wring their hands over all those little burn holes in our clothes and the reek of smoke that stayed with us. Sometimes in bed at night I could smell it, and I'd remember Bergy's face disappearing for a moment in the fog, the engine moving off down the tracks, the blurry, stinging eyes, and then the caboose—a point of reflected light in the distance, fading fast.

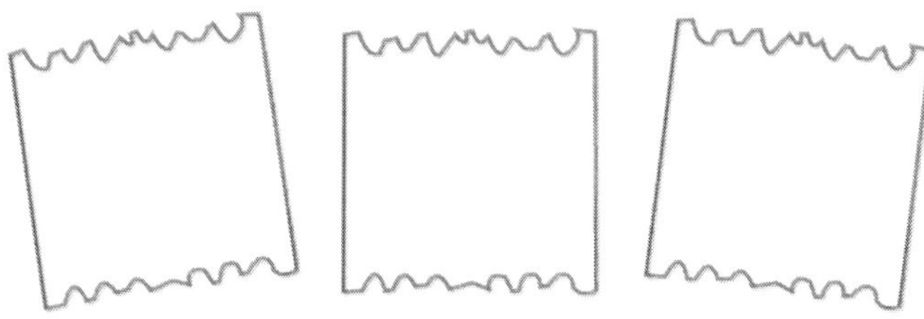

Door-to-Door

My mother didn't like me to answer he doorbell in our apartment because sometimes it was the Jehovah's Witnesses and she had a hard time getting rid of them because she didn't want to be rude. She even had a drawer full of their *Watchtower* magazines.

One time when my mother was giving my little sister a bath, I'd let the Property Tax lady in and when she asked about any new stuff we'd gotten, I showed her the new console TV set my father had recently surprised us with. After that, my mother said I could just wait till my father got home if I ever opened the door to a stranger again. That went double for salesmen, which we seemed to get a lot of, with everything from kitchen knives to encyclopedias. The one salesman my mother let in was the Fuller Brush man because she liked him and usually needed something he was selling, and if she didn't need anything, he was really good about leaving.

The only time I remember my father being home when a salesman came to the door was when he ended up buying this huge vacuum cleaner, which I really encouraged him to do because it had all kinds of special attachments, though I don't remember anybody ever using them. I was fascinated by that man, who even had a little bag of dirt he emptied on the rug just to show how well his vacuum cleaner could suck it up. He talked a lot about easy payments, too, which I was sure got my father interested, especially because of the way he was always complaining about anything he bought was too expensive.

Sometimes when I was playing with Bergy outside the apartment houses we'd see those salesmen in their suits and ties, sometimes lugging big suitcases up and down the stairs. Bergy said it looked like a pretty crummy job to have, even if he'd make a really good salesman himself, if he wanted to, and I had to agree with that. I also thought how bad I'd be at that job, standing outside someone's front door afraid to ring the bell—even if there was only some stupid kid waiting on the other side.

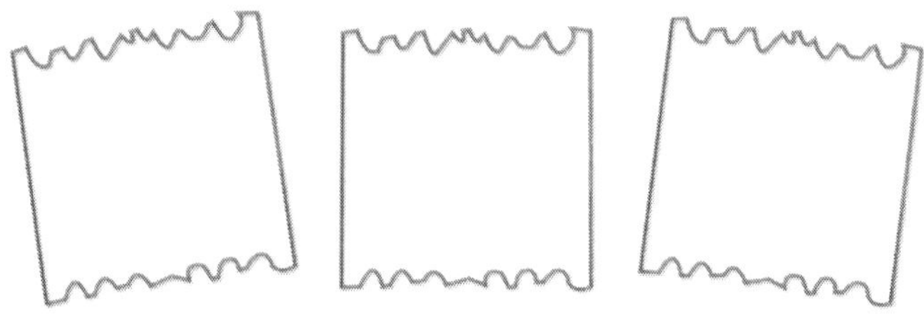

At the Movies
with Grownups

My parents were good friends of an older couple who didn't have any children, who sometimes stopped by for visits and were especially nice to me. One night when my father was away on a trip they decided to take me with them to the movies, which really made me excited because I loved movies more than just about anything. The only problem turned out to be the movie they wanted to see, which had a couple of pretty good parts but was mostly a boring love story and every once in awhile people would start singing and dancing. I kept waiting for something good to happen, trying hard to keep awake in that crowded theater where I felt strange being the only kid in sight. Things did get better on the way home when we stopped at Bridgeman's for chocolate sundaes, and when my mother asked me what I liked best about going to the movie and I said the ice cream, all of them had to chuckle.

I was used to people chuckling at me but it was almost impossible to imagine a movie I wouldn't like—the only one I could think of was my mother's favorite, *The Red Shoes*, which we saw one day when we were shopping downtown. The movie was about a woman who couldn't stop dancing when she wore these red shoes, and in the end she danced in front of a train and got killed. Even though my mother was crying she kept saying how much she loved that movie. That didn't make much sense to me, especially when it had made us both so sad.

It was a lot better when my father and mother took me to see *The Song of the South* at the RKO Orpheum theater downtown at night. It was mostly cartoons about a rabbit who kept tricking a fox and a bear, and I even liked the music. All the way home I kept singing the Zip-a-Dee-Doo-Dah song from the movie, watching all the lights and people through the car window. When I thought about it much later, what made me happiest was how much my parents seemed to like the movie too, even though I can't remember the three of us ever going to a movie together again.

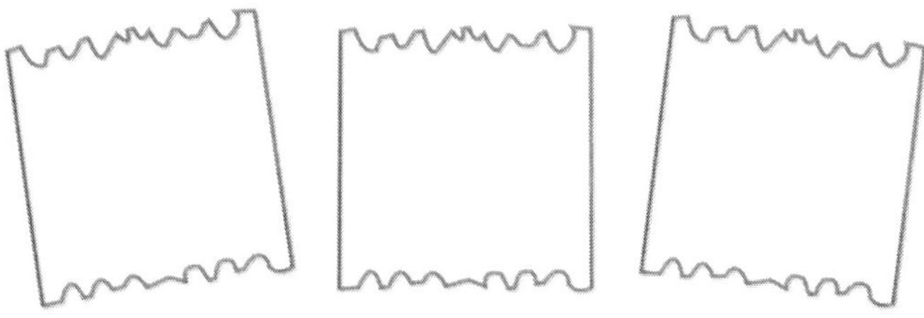

Looking Out for Me

Bergy knew some of the best tricks, like blowing your nose onto the grass by holding one nostril closed with your finger—except the first couple of times I tried it I got snot all over my shirt, which I had a hard time explaining to my mother. It was Bergy who showed me how to take apart my father's shotgun shells and light little trails of powder like they were fuses, and how to throw the butcher knife he'd swiped from his mother's kitchen drawer so it would stick into the big elm trees along the boulevard.

My mother probably got used to asking me if I had to do everything Bergy did, but at least she never told me she was sure I'd get hurt or that one of these days I'd learn my lesson. There were plenty of others around to do that, from my grandmother and my aunt to the old lady who lived in the house next door to our apartment and always called us filthy boys no matter what we were doing.

Sometimes I wondered if I ever stopped following Bergy's lead and did everything those women wanted me to do, if that would really satisfy them or make any difference in my life. Maybe I really was a sucker, which is what Bergy called me a lot—like after we'd been to the Saturday matinee at the Varsity and I was amazed by something I should have figured out. A lot of times I went along with what I saw on the screen because it was more fun that way. Even I could tell those robots were guys in metal suits and that there were wires holding the gun the Invisible Man aimed at Abbott and Costello. Sure, Flash Gordon's spaceship looked pretty fakey when it was supposed to be flying, you never saw any blood in those cowboy matinees even though a lot of guys got shot. Plus, how could the Lone Ranger get away with dressing like that when everyone else wore regular clothes?

That was one of the reasons I didn't always like going to the movies with Bergy. He kept reminding me about things I didn't really want to be thinking about, like it was his job or something. If I don't look out for you, who will?" Bergy always said. That seemed to be my problem—there were just too many people looking out for me, waiting for me to mess up.

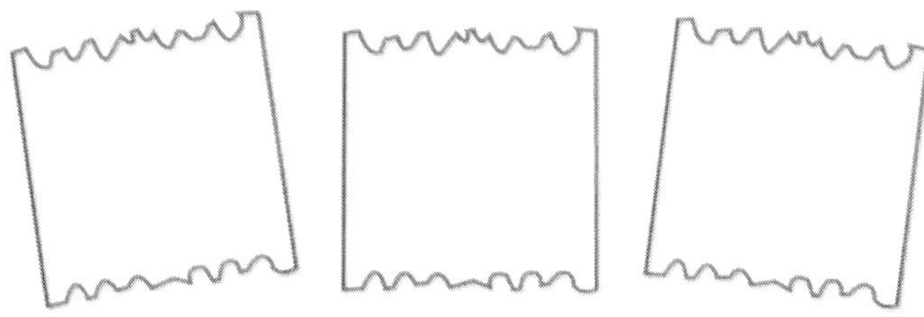

Head Wounds

There was blood on the floor and on my hand. At first I couldn't believe it came from me, sitting there holding the back of my throbbing head where it had slammed into the radiator by the cloakroom door.

The old wood floor was wet from all the kids coming in from recess on the snowy playground, and in the rush and shoving to get into our desks before the bell rang I'd slipped and fallen, as luck would have it, hitting the back of my head against the sharp edge of one of the radiator ridges. An accident, pure and simple, is what the principal said when they took me to his office to wait for my father to come and take me to the doctor. My head had finally stopped bleeding and hurting and I was brightening at the thought of having stitches to brag about. But I didn't even get to see the doctor—the nurse just put some medicine on the cut and said that head wounds always seemed a lot worse than they really were because of all that blood. By the time we left the doctor's office, school was nearly over for the day, so my father just dropped me off at home. About all he said in the car was that he hoped I'd learn to be a little more careful at school and that he wouldn't have to take time off from work again to come and get me.

When I went back to school on Monday, everyone seemed to have forgotten what had happened on Friday. It wasn't until recess when this girl named Annie came up to me and said she'd hoped I'd learned my lesson about acting so stupid, like I was Superman or something, when I jumped off that chair just before I fell against the radiator. I couldn't believe what she was saying. Didn't she know it wasn't really my fault if someone pushed me into the radiator? Didn't she realize I could have been seriously injured? After school when I told my friend Robert what Annie had said, he told me he couldn't believe I didn't remember what we'd been doing when we came in from recess and that I had been acting kind of weird.

On the way home I thought about what Robert said and then I got this really sick feeling, like someone had kicked me in the stomach. I finally remembered wrestling around with Paul Jackson and a couple of the other boys, pretending we were having a fist fight, when I got the bright idea to jump on them from a chair like I'd seen guys do in fights in cowboy movies. It all happened so quickly, and then with the excitement of all that blood I just must have just pushed it out of my head. And now I kept seeing Annie standing there on the playground, smirking at me and whispering to her friends, and even though nobody ever said anything again about my fall, I couldn't stop wondering how many of them really knew the truth.

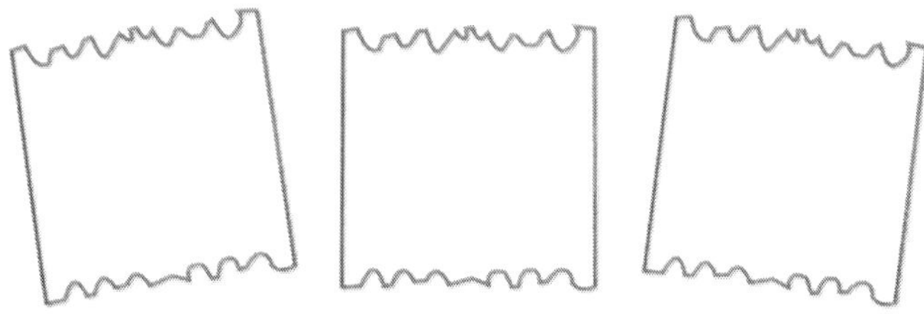

By the Numbers

One day our third grade teacher announced something she called a new policy. We couldn't just raise our hands anymore when we had to go to the bathroom. We had to raise fingers—one finger for making water, as she called it, and two fingers for the other thing. Most of us couldn't figure out what difference it made. A trip to the bathroom was a trip to the bathroom, after all, and if there was some reason why the teacher (and everyone else) had to know what we were up to, I could only chalk it up as another of those unsolvable classroom mysteries.

For the first couple of weeks the new policy didn't seem to make much of a difference. Most of the girls never raised their hands anyway, and nobody seemed to care what number a boy had to go—nobody, that is, but this small, bug-eyed kid named Roger who always kept to himself, and who most of us figured was about the dumbest one in the whole class. "Teacher, teacher," he'd cry out at least once a day, "I can't remember the difference between Number One and Number Two. Which one is for taking a leak?"

Sometimes the teacher would take Roger out in the hall to talk to him, where we could see his head bobbing like a yoyo behind the panes of glass in the door. When that happened, we knew he wouldn't be raising his hand again for at least a couple of days. But we also knew that soon enough he'd be at it again, and as the teacher's face got redder and redder we began to wonder just how long he could keep it up.

One day a week or so later, Paul Jackson, who was easily the most popular boy in class and also the best softball player, raised his hand and said the same thing, that he couldn't remember how many fingers to hold up. Then Buck Weiskopf asked the same question, followed by Freddie Johnson, and then the teacher told us all to put our heads down on our desks and not to say another thing. She also told us we were going to have a new policy, starting immediately. We'd have to write her a note about what we had to do in the bathroom and then bring it up to her desk when recognized us.

There new policy worked for about two days, until Roger raised his hand and asked the teacher how many *r*'s there were in "urinate" so he could write it on his note. That was the only time we'd ever heard a teacher scream. It was when we also knew that from then on we'd have to start holding it till recess— and that Roger wasn't nearly as stupid as we'd all thought he was.

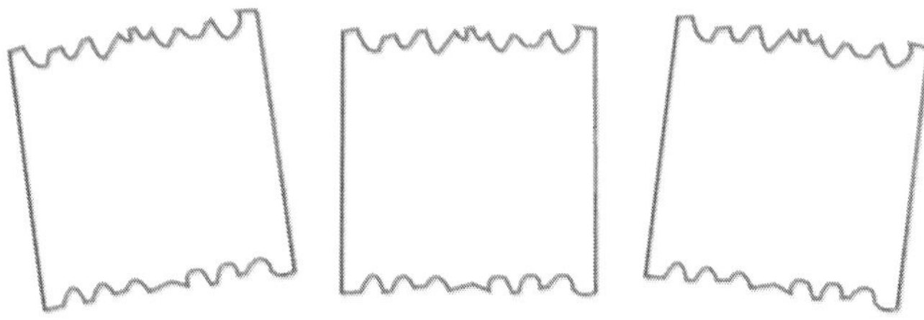

The Invisible Enemy

Our neighborhood had several old woodpiles, usually out by the alleys and half-grown over with weeds. There wasn't just wood there but anything the garbage men wouldn't take, which made them great places for kids—even if parents regularly warned us what could happen if we got jabbed by a rusty nail.

The nearest woodpile was behind the garages where nobody from the apartments could see us playing. It was always good for the apple crates we'd knock apart for whatever we decided to build, which most of the time didn't turn out to be anything we wanted to keep. And once in awhile we'd find a real treasure, like dials and switches from an old short wave radio which we used for the control panel of our rocket ship, or an old gas can with a little of the gas still inside. Mostly, it was a meeting place, and one where some of the best games started, like "the devil in the dark," which was a line from some war movie we'd seen at the Varsity Theater. It had to do with an enemy airplane which everyone was afraid of because it made sneak attacks on Navy ships at night. So, when someone screamed out "devil in the dark" we'd all climb up on the woodpile like it was our ship to defend and start shooting our guns, which were usually made out of old boards. Even if it was only Bergy and me by ourselves, and even if we weren't anywhere near the woodpile, we still liked to say it, especially when someone's mother started calling that it was time to come in. "Devil in the dark," we'd scream, scrambling to our gun positions and then falling in the grass and laughing our heads off.

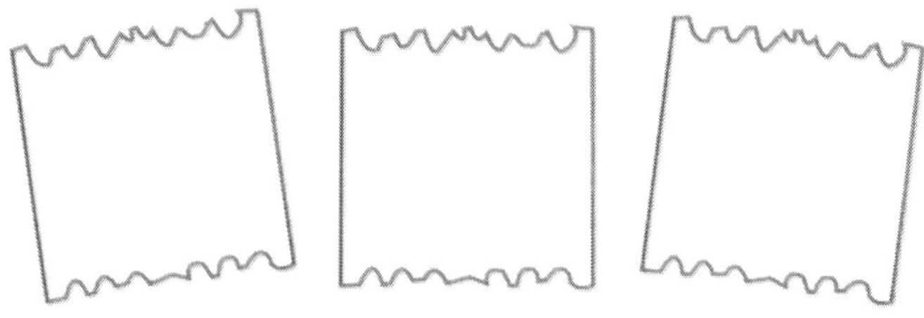

Hopeless Case

In our apartment house, Bergy had the corner on emptying trash for all the old ladies. Each day I'd watch him hauling bags out back to the garbage cans and incinerator, and then on Saturday morning he'd collect his money—right before we'd head off to the matinee at the Varsity. "Buck twenty-five this week," he'd say, rubbing his hands together. "That's not counting tips." "Tips of *what?*" I asked once, and Bergy just rolled his eyes.

Once when I was sick or maybe just too lazy, my mother even paid Bergy to empty *our* trash. That meant no movies on Saturday for me, no candy either. "Sorry to do this to you," Bergy said, "but business is business." Who was I to argue? Bergy had a bank account. He had a paper route, too, ran errands up and down the block, stole all the empty pop bottles off the back porches before I even knew they were there. I was probably home waiting for our wastebaskets to fill up, hoping one of my teeth might somehow fall out—anything would do, as long as I had money for Saturday.

"Spend it all again this week?" Bergy would say, which is just what my father said. What did they know anyway? *All* of them who frowned at me, jingling their stupid pockets—jingling, jingling, jingling as they walked away.

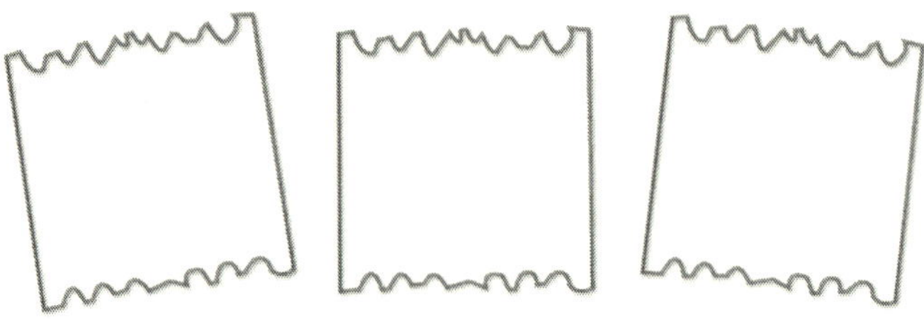

Trick or Treat

"Good teeth run in my family," Bergy told me. He'd never had a filling at the dentist's office, even if he ate just as much candy as I did. He'd laugh when I tried to tell him about that terrifying drill. He really laughed when I told him about the time the lady at the dentist's office popped out three of my rotten baby teeth when she was flossing me.

"You didn't even bring them home with you?" Bergy said. "That's twenty-five cents apiece you blew." I couldn't figure his arithmetic—*my* tooth fairy only paid a dime. "Tooth fairy?" Bergy said. "You know your old man is the tooth fairy, don't you?" And then he started in on Santa Claus and the Easter Bunny.

It was hard to figure, all that stuff Bergy told me—at least he didn't ruin Halloween. My bellyache did that, after we'd eaten all our candy in one sitting, as my mother put it. Actually, we were standing out behind the garages when I started to feel it, drunk with candy—all my teeth going rotten at once. But this time I was going to pull them out myself, long before that dentist's lady ever got hold of me. And then I was going to have a talk with my father about the going rate for teeth under my pillow.

"Sure you will, Bergy said," flashing me another of his perfect grins.

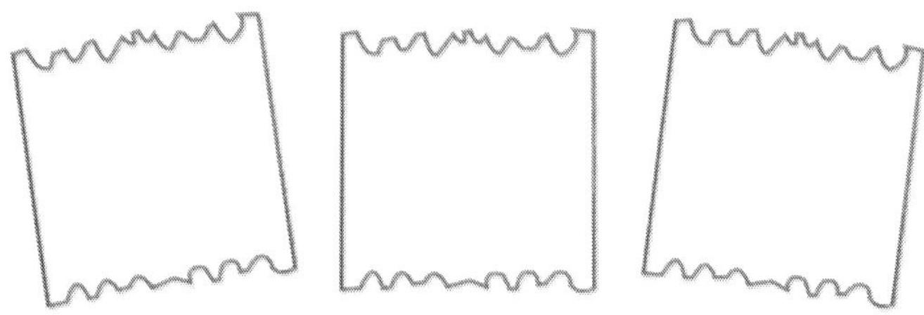

Entrepreneur

Bergy decided we had to have a Kool-Aid stand—if I'd get my mother to make the Kool-Aid, that is; if I could get her to loan us the card table, and buy some paper cups. He'd take care of the money. He'd even make a sign if I could find some old paint in the garage—oh, and a brush, too, and a big piece of cardboard. He'd see if he could swipe some masking tape.

There we sat on the corner the two hottest, muggiest days of August—Dog Days, my mother called them, though we didn't see any dogs and not many people either. Just a couple of nuns from the little convent a block away. Bergy called them penguins, but not me. I didn't dare to. And I didn't dare to tell him how much they scared me or how sometimes they'd show up in my bad dreams. Most of the time, it seemed, those nuns were watching us from across the street.

Oh, a car stopped once to ask directions, and our fathers each bought a glass or two when they came home from work, but mostly all we had to show for our efforts were the red rings around our mouths. "Get your cherry beer, five cents a glass," Bergy would shout to the nuns, and then he'd disappear for awhile—he had to help his mother with the wash, he said, or run an errand for his aunt.

I never told Bergy that one time when he left, two of those old penguins finally crossed the street and bought two glasses of Kool-aid without even speaking to me, or how my hand shook when I reached out for that warm, damp dime the tall one fished out from somewhere in all that black she wore. I never told him either how I dreamed that I was going straight to hell, or how I kept that dime hidden in my pocket, for weeks—where I could feel it from time to time, slowly burning that hole I'd been warned about.

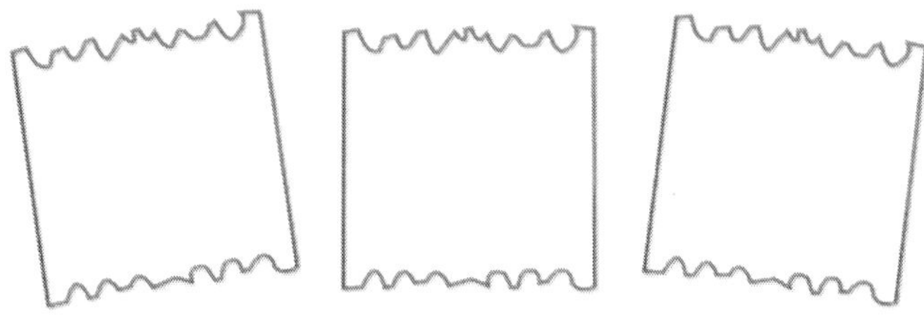

Sex Education

We saw them floating in the gutter on a rainy day—three balloons, I thought, but Bergy said not to pick them up. "You don't know anything," he said. "Those are rubbers, what men put on their wieners. You want to touch something like that?" Bergy knew a lot when it came to men and women, knew about morfadikes and why they kept those jars of dead babies in the zoology lab at the university, the place we'd sometimes sneak into on Saturdays. What he didn't know was about my grandfather's medical book my cousin and I had discovered one day during summer vacation. The skin diseases were the worst, the woman with a baby coming out of her a close second.

We never found a morfadike in the book—I did tell Bergy that—and rubbers weren't there either. "Who's your friend," Bergy said, "me or that stupid book?" I had to wonder where Bergy got his information, even if he *was* older, had his own room and comic books my mother didn't even want me to know about. One thing's for certain when it came to Bergy—I never knew what dark, goose-bumpy thing he'd tell me next. And someday, I was hoping, he'd have to get to the most important things. He'd have to tell me why.

Slow Learner

"It's time you learned how to smoke," Bergy said. His old man puffed on a pipe so it was up to me to swipe a cigarette from mine. "What if he counts them?" I asked. "Don't be a girl," Bergy said, which is the thing I didn't want to be. So, late that night when I couldn't sleep I took a Raleigh cork-tip from the pack on the kitchen table. "I like Luckies better," Bergy said, "but I suppose this will do the trick." What trick was that? The way I coughed and rubbed my burning eyes, or the way I threw up on the basement steps? And how had Bergy ever gotten me to that dark old basement where we both knew there were rats?

"Just like I thought," Bergy said. "You're a girl." And then he told everyone at school the way my face turned green and I puked. "It was the rats," I lied. "I saw a rat when we were down there." Even Bergy was afraid to mess with rats. That's when he started calling me Rat Boy. I couldn't even tell my mother, knowing I'd get a licking if she found out I was down the basement with Bergy. Well, maybe it wasn't so bad being Rat Boy, I kept telling myself. At least I wasn't a girl.

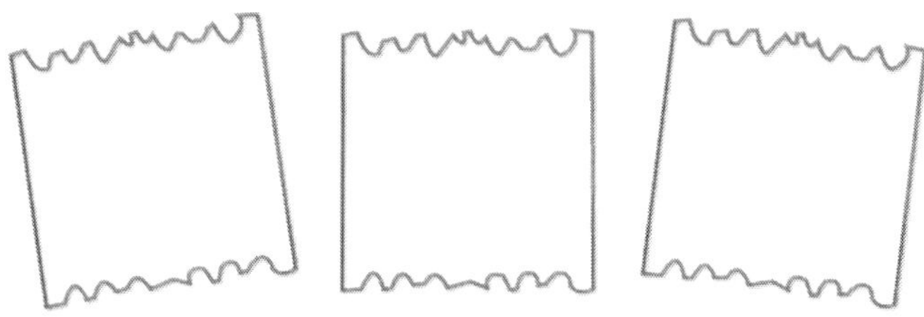

Special Offers

The best thing about breakfast was cereal that had prizes buried in it, like the little plastic spacemen in the box of Raisin Bran. There were always boxtops to be collected for special offers, too, or labels like the one from the jar of Ovaltine, or O-Valentine as my grandfather called it. I worked hard for weeks to get my mother to buy it so I could order my secret decoder for the Captain Midnight program on the radio. But when it finally came, the messages I decoded were usually pretty stupid and the Ovaltine tasted terrible.

When I asked Bergy if he had a decoder too, so we could at least send secret messages to each other, he said that was baby stuff and didn't interest him—what we really needed were walkie-talkies, which I already knew my mother would tell me we just couldn't afford. Worse yet, whenever I asked her to buy some new kind of cereal, especially the kind with sugar already added, she'd ask me if I'd like a cup of Ovaltine, which was another way of reminding me that no matter what it tasted like I was expected to use up what my parents had paid good money for. There it sat, almost full, right next to the boxes of cereal—one that I'd already fished the prize out of and would have to wait a long time to have replaced, and one that my father liked, the corn flakes which didn't promise anything at all.

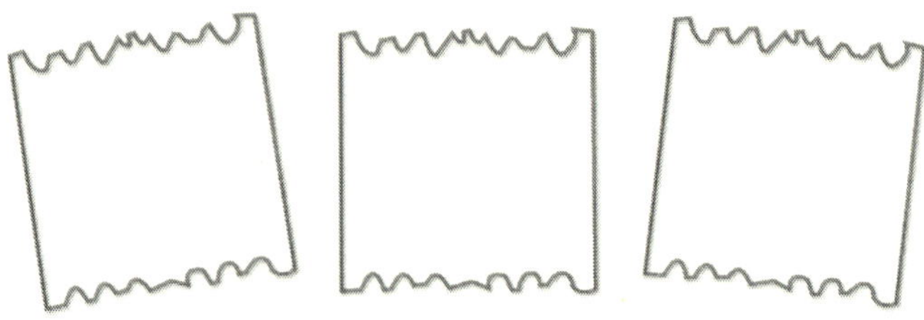

Saving Up

More than anything, I wanted a new fielder's glove, but my mother said we'd have to wait until we had enough Raleigh coupons. Half our apartment, it seemed, came from coupons or stamps—S&H Green Stamps or Gold Bond Stamps and some others I can't even remember. Sometimes I'd sit there and finger those fat books of stamps and piles of coupons held together with rubber bands, imagining they were real money and what I was going to buy with them. There wasn't much in those catalogs that interested me— dishes, toasters, floorlamps, stuff for my baby sister. Besides, we had most of it already.

The Raleigh catalog did have a fielder's glove, and even if it wasn't quite what I had in mind I knew it was the only one I had a chance of getting. "Right after we get the last chair for the card table," my father told me. That's what he'd been saving up for so that had to come first.

I asked all my friends if their fathers smoked Raleigh cigarettes but none of them did, though Bergy told me he was getting a catcher's mitt for his birthday and his father didn't even smoke cigarettes.

I'd just have to be patient, my mother said. Besides, it wouldn't be baseball season for another couple of months. I knew my father couldn't smoke enough in that short time to get all the coupons we'd need for that fielder's glove. It'd be Halloween if I was lucky, but that was when l was hoping for a new football.

"You can't get something for nothing," my mother said. I tried to remember that each time I saw her licking stamps when she got home from the grocery store, each time I saw my father lighting up a cigarette. How old did I have to be, anyway, before I got as smart as they were?

Sweet Tooth

There was a wooden ledge running around the dining room wall, which I could barely reach standing on a chair, and sometimes when I climbed up to check it, I'd find a penny or nickel, which I'd take to the little store across the street from school for candy. It never occurred to me that I was actually stealing that money—not when it came to buying candy, anyway.

When I was a little older, my mother would send me to the store on errands, and I usually got to keep a little of the change. I always meant to save up and buy something that would please my parents, but that never happened—all that penny candy and bubblegum were too tempting to resist. But one day I did have a chance for something more than penny candy. One day I came into more money than I'd ever seen before.

I'd taken a shortcut across the lawn in front of the high school and I came across a whole pile of loose change in the grass, where someone had been sitting, probably not very long before I walked by. But there was no one in sight, and I suddenly understood the meaning of "finders keepers." I thought for a while about what I could use that money for—a present for my mother, maybe, or some of my very own comic books, which would really impress Bergy, even if I'd have to keep them hidden from my parents. But then I thought of an even better way to show Bergy that there was something I could do and he couldn't, and that was to take him for a Coke at the drugstore soda fountain.

The trouble was, I couldn't stop with just one. "Ever tried a cherry Coke?" Bergy asked. So, we did. And then a lime Coke and a chocolate Coke and some others I couldn't even remember by the time I got home. But there was candy, too—Good and Plenty and Root Beer Barrels, like we'd sometimes get at the Saturday matinee at the Varsity theater. I couldn't keep myself from buying more.

For the next few days we kept talking and laughing about what a good time we'd had at the drug store and how next time it would have to be Bergy's turn to treat. Being what Bergy called a big spender had made me feel wonderful, especially for finally outdoing him at something. What made me feel bad was when I counted what was left of my treasure there wasn't nearly enough for a present for my mother or even a couple of comic books. And then I thought how angry my father would be with me for wasting money, though he might understand the Coke and candy. He always said he had a sweet tooth, since he liked to put sugar on everything, like tomatoes and bread and butter sandwiches. Maybe I had one too. That might explain what I'd done with that money, and with all the coins I'd found at home, too. I could only hope that my sweet tooth would be one I'd be losing with the rest of my baby teeth. But I also knew the aching I kept feeling inside wasn't from anything as simple as a rotten tooth.

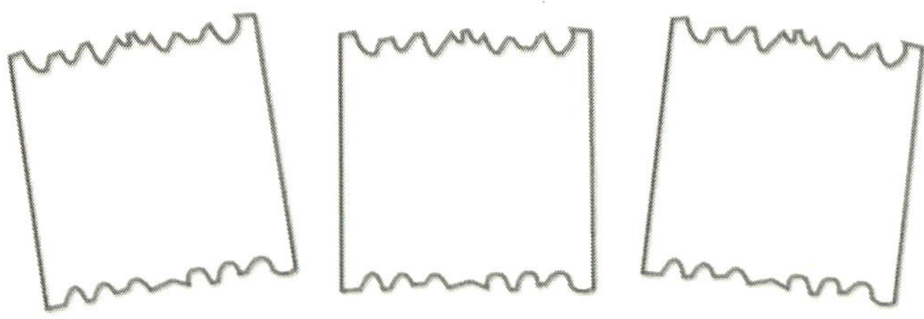

The Bad Seed

When my parents made me go to Sunday school, my mother always asked when I got home just what I'd learned. Nothing, I'd say. They told some stupid stories, like that one about farming. Some of the kids pretended it was a big deal, but what did I care about *crops*, anyway—the good seed springing forth to golden wheat for harvest while the weeds got burned? Or how about those baskets of bread and fish the teacher—who wasn't really a teacher, just a high school girl—talked about in her chirpy voice. She slapped these little felt cutouts on a cloth-covered board as if we needed them to understand about multitudes and miracles, and I got in trouble when she heard me say that I'd bet *she* wouldn't want to eat that stuff for supper.

What I really learned was that I hated sermons, even if they fed you afterwards, and that there were people I wanted to punch in the face because they'd pretend to go along with anything. Someday I might even be brave enough to keep on walking past those huge church doors on Sunday morning, over to my favorite place—that vacant lot where there was no wheat, where the only things springing forth were weeds and grasshoppers, where nobody cared about miracles or anything else I didn't understand.

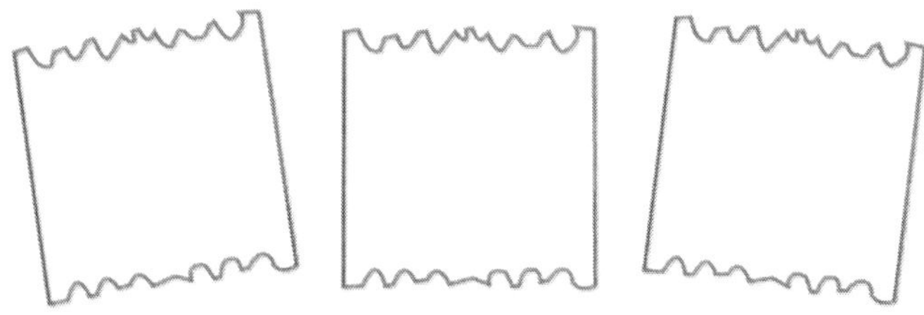

A Zoo Story

One of the best times I could imagine was a trip to the big zoo at Como Park, which was a pretty long drive from home. I must have asked my father just about every weekend he was home in nice weather if we could go to the zoo again, but with grocery shopping with my mother on Saturdays and all kinds of things that needed to get done around the apartment, he didn't take us out very often except maybe on a Sunday afternoon to visit our friends the Johnsons who lived out by the airport. Still, once a year or so my father would give in and we'd head to the zoo, where at first I'd run like a maniac from pen to pen shouting out the wonderful names, like African Crown Crane or Mongolian Musk Ox. There were polar bears, too, keeping cool in their little pool, and giraffes and gazelles and a lot of other animals I'd seen in movies. Then there was the strangest place and the smelliest, Monkey Island, where people would try to throw pieces of bread or fruit across the moat and where some of the monkeys were doing things to each other that embarrassed me and I didn't even know why.

We usually saved the best for last—the gorillas, though they always seemed to be asleep in the far corners of their cages, and the big cats, who did nothing else but pace back and forth behind the bars. When you could see their eyes they looked a little crazy. That's when I was ready to go home. In the back seat of the car with my little sister asleep next to me, I'd think a lot about those lions and tigers and leopards pacing in their little cages and then about some of the other animals who looked unhappy too. I had to wonder how I could forgot something like that that since our last visit to the zoo, but deep down I also knew I'd probably forget it again by the next time I'd start asking my father when we could go again.

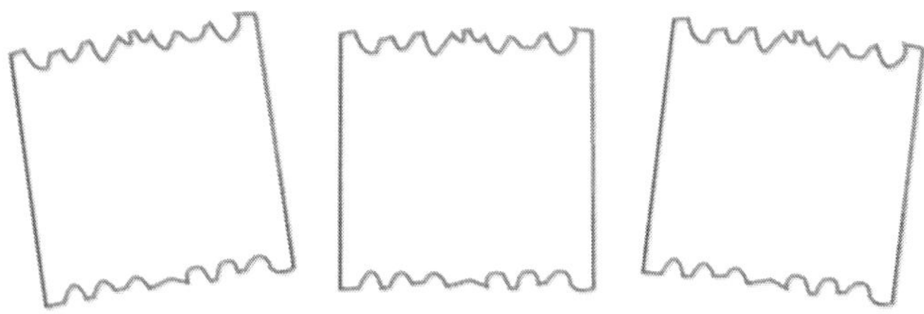

Tax Time

I can remember more than once the night my father covered the kitchen or the dining room table with pens and pencils, shoe boxes full of receipts, and other papers of all sizes and colors, and my mother warning me to be especially quiet, to keep out of sight if at all possible because taxes were due and my father would probably be up most of the night.

I didn't have much of an idea of what taxes were all about except that they involved money my father had to pay the government or he'd be in big trouble. To see my father sweating in his undershirt, chain smoking and scratching his head gave me bad dreams about the government. It's a little like that schoolwork you know you have to do and sometimes put off till the last minute anyway, my mother told me once, but I couldn't imagine any teacher doing to me what the government was doing to my father. And then I thought about having to pay taxes myself, and I really felt hopeless. Someday the government would be coming after me, and it looked like the only way I could stop it was to figure out some way never to grow up.

Crime & Punishment

Everybody knew it wasn't very hard to swipe something from the little five and dime in our neighborhood. Some of the boys in my room at school used to make a game of it—plastic cars, baseball cards, comic books. The only kid I ever saw get caught was swiping comic books. I used to dream about the man who ran the store dragging him off to some back room. That kid just looked at me standing in the aisle with my hands in my pockets, as if to say he knew that I was guilty too. I had to be.

Well, I wasn't—not then anyway. Bergy said that kid would probably go to prison but it wouldn't be as bad as what his parents did to him. Maybe if I took something for my sister it wouldn't count. Any little thing would do, just to show the boys at school. It wasn't enough anymore to take the nickels I'd find around the apartment for candy and gum. I had to take that little doll, inside my stocking cap. Nothing to it, I bragged to my school friends—who were expecting something more. The hard part was putting it back the next day, just after the dime store man stopped me to ask how my father was doing. How did he know my father, anyway? And who else did he know?

Bergy didn't believe me when I told him what I'd done. No one did. But it didn't matter. I knew I wouldn't be swiping anything else from that five and dime. I knew too that my mother probably left those nickels out on purpose. I could feel it in the grownups, all of them—everything I thought I understood and didn't. Everything I thought I'd hidden, written all over my guilty little face.

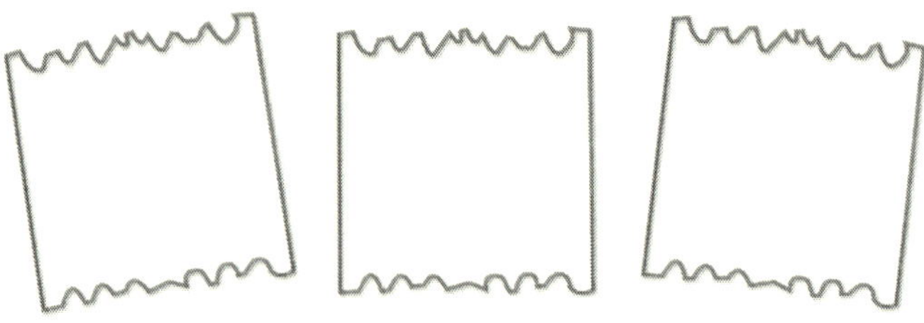

Higher Education

Bergy liked to remind me that his father had some kind of important job at the university, which was only a few blocks away. Sometimes the two of us pulled our wagons over there, looking for pop bottles we could turn in at the House of Hansen for two cents apiece, and in the fall during Homecoming, some of the guys at the fraternity houses would give us crepe paper to decorate our wagons. Living in a fraternity house looked like it might be fun, but as for the university itself—or "the U," as most people called it—we didn't have much of an idea what really went on there, except that students had to be pretty smart. It had a lot of different buildings with names on them like Physics or Archaeology, which Bergy said was his favorite because it was all about fossils, which he and his father used to find in rocks on their hikes down by the Mississippi River. The fossils he showed me looked like little seashells or leaves pressed into those rocks, which weren't very interesting to me, even if he made a big deal about the special hammer he'd gotten for his fossil hunting.

Bergy was certain that one day he was going to the U, maybe to study archaeology, and that it was too bad I didn't know what I wanted to do when I got bigger. I thought about that a lot and started to wonder which of those buildings I'd be going to if I ever went to the U, and what I was going to do if I couldn't find one with something I wanted to study. Bergy said not to worry about it too much. I could do lots of things when I grew up that didn't depend on going to the U, but I knew that if Bergy was going, then I was too. There had to be more of those buildings somewhere, and one of them had the name of something I'd be really interested in—even if I had to wander around a long time before I found it.

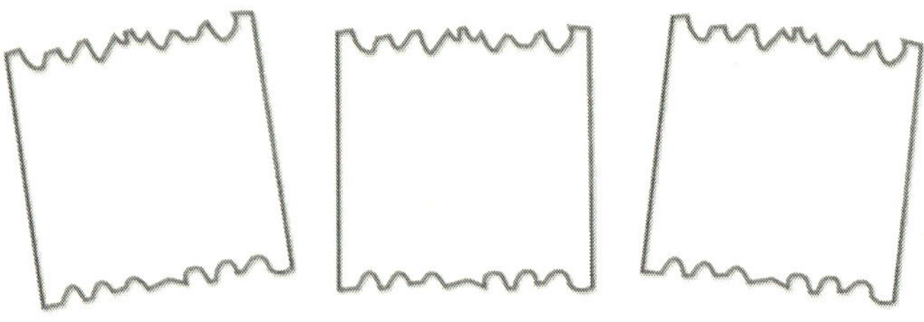

Dog Days

The worst part of summer, when it got really hot and sticky, was what my mother called Dog Days. I guessed the name came from someone watching a dog panting, and that's the way I felt—too hot to move, with my own tongue hanging out all the way to the floor.

For some reason Dog Days always made me think of school, too, maybe because they'd usually come in August, when summer suddenly didn't seem to have much left to it. It was a time when a lot of people went on vacation, too, so the neighborhood was especially quiet, though I could till see fans turning in a lot of windows, and the old man who lived upstairs across from us would be sitting out on his balcony every night because it was too hot to go inside. Bergy always called him by his first name, which was Luke, though my parents said I should always call grownups mister or missus. Bergy liked to call everyone by their first names, even his parents, and no one seemed to mind.

Bergy was usually gone on vacation with his family during Dog Days, which meant I had to spend more time than usual being bored. The only thing I liked about them was watching the heat lightning, as my father called it, just about every night. It wasn't the kind of lightning you had to be afraid of, like when a big storm was coming, and no one ever went inside because of it. If it did get around to raining it wouldn't be till after I was in bed. I'd lie awake and listen to the rain sometimes—a gentle sound that made me feel snug, even if it was still too hot to sleep. Then I'd hear my parents talking in the kitchen or maybe just my father, who seemed to have as much trouble sleeping as I did. I knew he'd be sitting there at the table in the dark, fiddling with the radio or maybe having a bowl of cereal. And once in awhile I'd hear people from somewhere far away, laughing or calling to each other out in the street, and that made me think about something I'd really wanted to do, like going to the State Fair, or maybe on a long train trip to one of those places I'd read about, like the Grand Canyon. Just about anything seemed possible then, as the lightning kept the sky flashing, changing night to day.

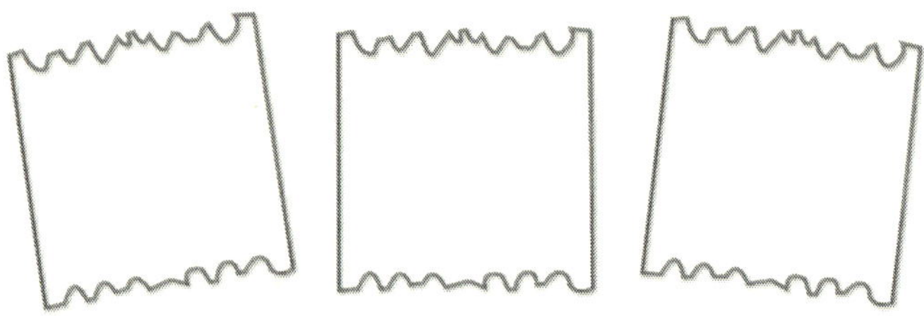

No Picnic

Whenever we'd go on trips in the car—which were always to visit relatives—my mother would pack us a picnic lunch in a big basket with a lid. Mostly there'd be cheese and summer sausage sandwiches, some kind fruit and cookies, and a thermos of coffee for her and my father, and one of Kool Aid for my sister and me. It was pretty much what we had for lunch at home. The times I'd ride with my grandparents to their town in North Dakota there'd be a lot of different things, like pieces of fried chicken and a bowl of potato salad or watermelon slices, but then they usually seemed to eat a lot better than we did.

When I was riding with my family and it got close to noon, my father would tell me to start looking for a good place to stop for lunch, which usually was a picnic table at some little park or roadside stop. But he always carried a blanket in the trunk, too, for the times we couldn't find a table—for some uncomfortable grassy place my parents would talk about like it was Yellowstone Park.

To my parents, those picnics on trips always seemed to be some special kind of fun, but to me the real fun would be eating in a café or restaurant. My mother said we took picnics because my father had to eat in cafés all the time when he was traveling for his job, but I suspected it was because cafés would cost too much money. She also told me she couldn't understand why I didn't like to eat outside—as if she could forget there would usually be flies or bees or mosquitoes, sometimes so bad we'd have to go back an eat in the car. When I grew up and went on trips I knew I was never going to eat my lunch outside. I'd eat in cafés, or better yet, drive-ins, like the A&W Root Beer drive-in I remembered seeing once, framed like a picture in the rear window of the car.

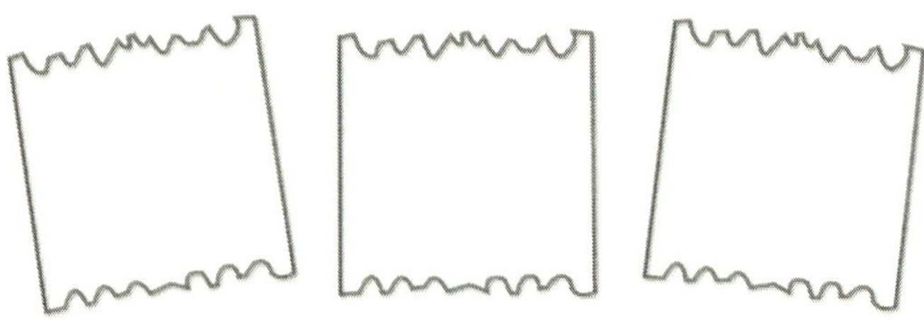

The Fat Kid

When my waist size was getting close to the same as my father's, he told me he was getting concerned. "Baby fat" was what my Aunt Molly called it, assuring him that one day I'd lose it just like I was losing my baby teeth. What I heard from the old woman who lived downstairs and sometimes invited me in for milk and cookies was, "Will your mother let you eat this? You'd better go upstairs and check." "The kid's turning into a lummox," my father said. He had a different way with words.

I sometimes daydreamed they'd invent a blubber machine to strip away the fat, or that someday I'd find a loose thread in my belly, and when I tugged it all those pounds would unravel like a bulky sweater. Fat kids had to believe in science and magic, in mothers who loved them, in second helpings that don't count if nobody sees you take them, in fathers who were mostly gone on trips.

Lardass, blimp, and fatty, fatty two-by-four, I heard them all. Each class I was in had mostly skinny kids—how did they do it, anyway? Someday I'd know. Someday I'd find the secret thread. Someday I'd go back and tell that grinning old woman what she could do with her cookies. Someday, when they didn't taste so good.

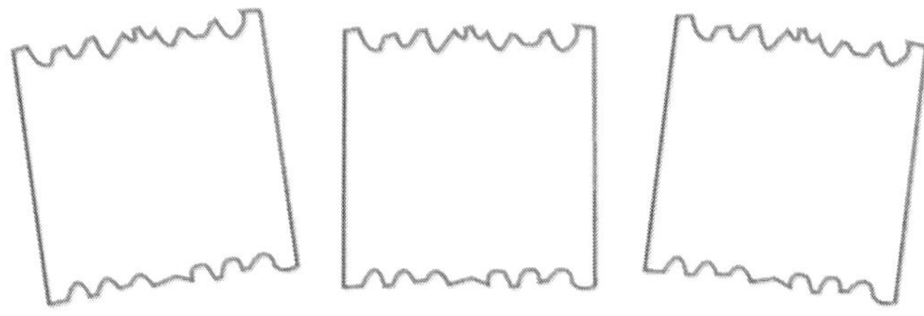

Stamps of Approval

My father collected stamps when he was a boy—he showed me his album full of strange-looking ones I couldn't believe weren't worth a fortune—and together we got started on the album he gave me for Christmas. What I cared most about were those gaudy triangles and diamonds outlined on some of the pages—the ones I knew it was hard to find, except maybe in those little packets in the hobby store, which I couldn't begin to afford. My father never bought pre-packaged stamps except for those cheap mixed selections, almost all of which were the most common ones. Still, I kept hoping I'd discover something good in those jam-packed envelopes, but the best I ever found were some uncancelled three-centers which my mother said she'd use on letters.

I knew it made my father happy to see my album spread open on my desk, along with those little tweezers and magnifying glass and packet of stamp hinges. So, that's where I kept it, long after I'd given up ever being a collector, much less finding a stamp that was worth a fortune, like the one I'd heard about with the airplane printed upside down. When I checked some stamp books out of the library, too, I found that none of the stamps in my father's album were worth more than 50 cents, and even at that, who was going to buy them? The guy at the hobby store said the best place was at the annual stamp show in Chicago. He might as well have said on the moon.

Every once in awhile my father and I would sit down with our albums at the dining room table, especially after my grandparents had sent a big envelope of stamps from their travels. Once, I asked my father if *his* father had collected stamps too, but he said he never really knew his father—he had been killed by a train when my father was still a little boy.

After that, I made it a point to ask more often if we could work on stamps together. Even if my father didn't usually have the time, and even if we really weren't making much progress on those albums, I guessed it might be important to keep asking.

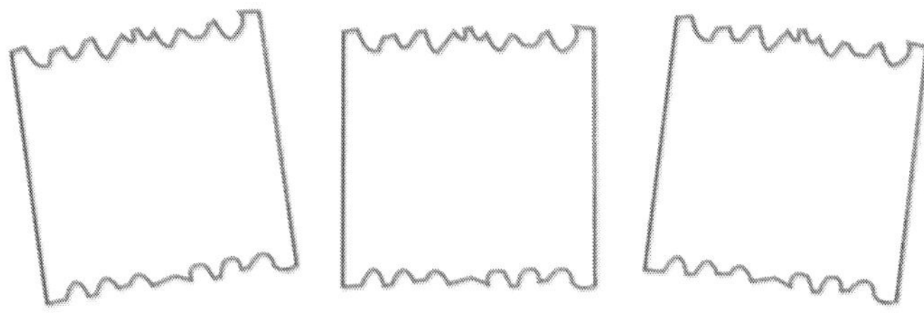

Family Secret

Some of us never survived the Depression, my grandmother used to tell me. I never knew what that meant until the time we left on summer vacation and my father tried to stretch a tank of gas because it was a few cents cheaper in St. Cloud. When we ran out, it was two miles from town and right next to the state reformatory. My father trudged off along the road, head down, while my mother and I watched the walls, the guard turrets watching us. I was sure there'd be a break any minute, sure those desperate convicts would come to get us. I'd seen some prison movies, after all, and we were in real danger. My only bright thought was that somehow it would serve my father right.

While my mother and my little sister napped, I kept watch, waiting for the worst, until my father came back riding in a gas station truck with a can of his precious St. Cloud gas, and my mother said I should try to understand he'd had to pay a lot more than he bargained on. But I didn't I know much about paying or about saving pennies or surviving, either. And I kept waiting for my father to say something about what happened, but he never did.

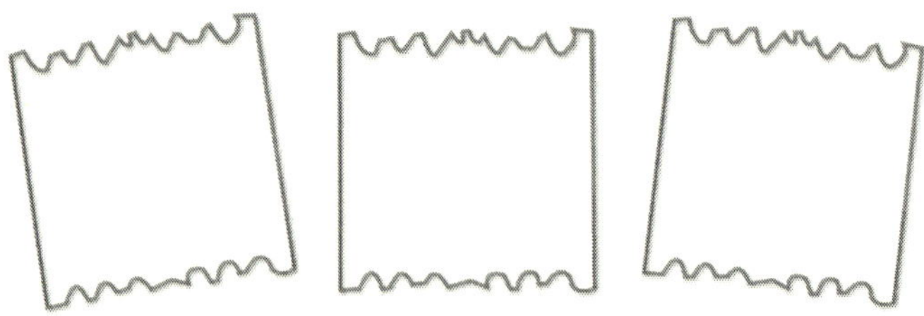

Home Fires

Both of my parents grew up in small towns, and even if living in the city didn't bother them, they seemed a lot happier whenever we visited their hometowns every summer, especially my mother's over in North Dakota. What amazed me most about that place was that there was only one of just about everything—drug store, bank, hardware store, grocery store, movie theater. Everybody seemed to have a garden, too, where the women spent most of the afternoon and where I'd help from time to time, picking strawberries for shortcake or jam, which I loved, or tomatoes, which sometimes I picked too green so my grandmother would line them up to ripen on the sunny window sill. My only real job was to pump a pail of cold water each day from the well across the street. It tasted much better than the water from the house, which my grandmother said was softened—which didn't make much sense to me. I also got to walk to the post office downtown to pick up the mail each afternoon about an hour after the mail train came rumbling through.

Even though my grandfather had retired he still kept an office downtown so he could visit his friends. He liked to sing—mostly hymns, like *This Is My Story*—and play rummy, too, and he taught me at least seven different kinds of solitaire, which helped pass the afternoons when there weren't any other kids around. He also paid me for cutting the grass with the old pusher lawnmower, which had a basket I had to empty about every two minutes. A couple of times when I didn't get the job done on time, my grandfather just did it himself and didn't say anything, though my grandmother really lit into me about how lazy and ungrateful I was, which probably came from living in the city, and how things were different here—maybe one day I'd understand that.

And one day I did. A song my grandfather taught me started out, "Keep the home fires burning," which bothered me the first time I heard it because I thought it was about burning houses. But then he told me what it really meant and I remembered it for a long time, knowing that even if I was from the city and sometimes pretty thoughtless, there was always something for me right there, burning bright.

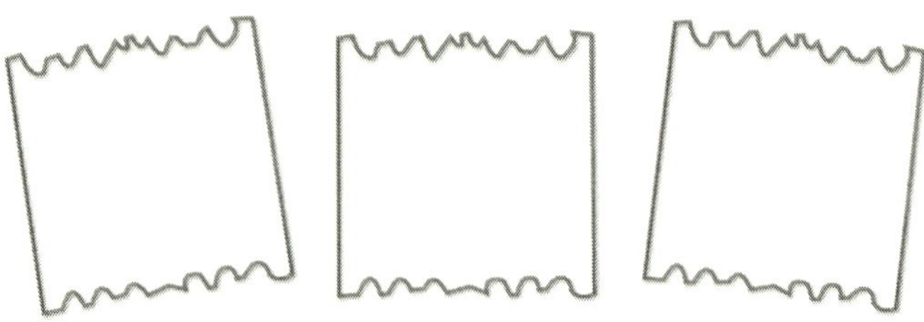

Sparklers

Once in awhile my mother's family had a summer reunion at my grandparents'
house in their small town—a few aunts and uncles and a lot of cousins I had
a hard time keeping straight. It was usually on the 4th of July, after a big picnic
and just before the fireworks at the County Fair—out in the backyard, where
the grownups sat around in lawnchairs and the kids twirled their sparklers in
loops and zigzags. *Look!* we shouted to the grownups, afraid they'd somehow
miss the bright slash of every turn and leap, until the last glow died and
we'd go back for more, warned each time about burned hands and bare feet
slipping in the dewy grass. *Again!* we yelled, and ran as far beyond the porch
lights as we dared, for this was Independence Day and we were too busy to
listen, writing our names in thin air.

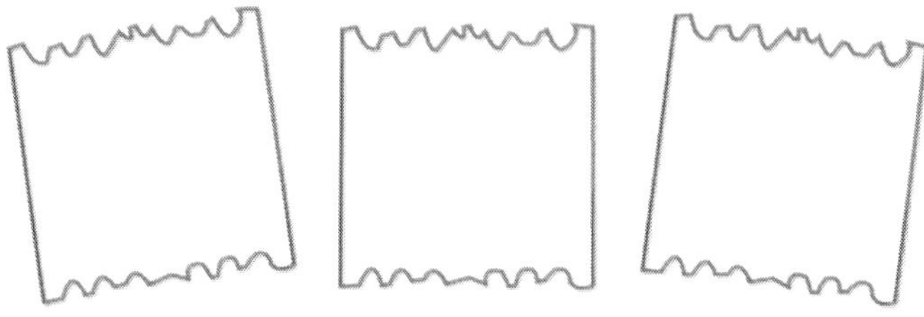

The Last Day of Summer

I couldn't understand why no one worked on something called Labor Day, but then, I'd expected Coca Cola at the pops concert my uncle and aunt took me to. When I thought about it, I had to admit I was lucky they made a holiday out of it, holding off the start of school for one more day at least. The only part I used in the diary my grandmother gave me was the little calendar, checking off the remaining days left summer vacation like a condemned man. By the time August showed up, I'd start dreading school again—I couldn't seem to stop thinking about it.

Labor Day was also the end of the State Fair, which was so much bigger and more expensive than the little county fair in my grandparents' town. I only got to go on a couple of rides, and once, with Bergy, who we'd taken along and who surprised me by rocking the Ferris wheel seat when we got to the top because I had told him it really bothered me. But when we knew it was the last trip around, both of us just sat and stared off into the darkness above all the Midway lights and didn't say a thing, just hanging up there where nobody could touch us, before those big gears grabbed again and we lurched toward teachers and tests and all the rest that seemed rising up to meet us.

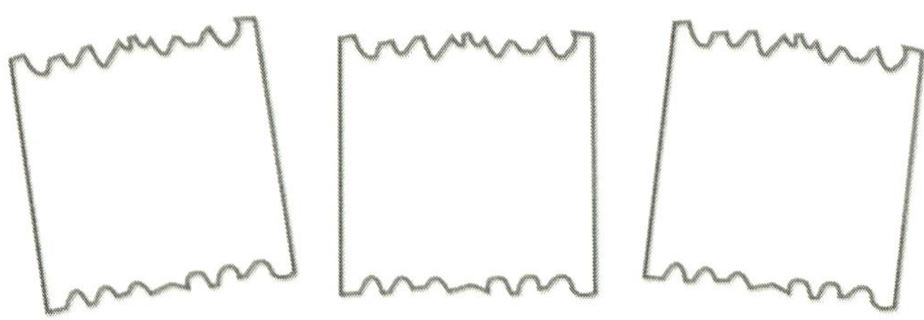

Mysteries

Ever since our teacher read us *Lad, a Dog* I dreamed of having my own pet. The only problem with dogs was that they didn't seem to like me. Even though Marcy School was only a block walk from where I lived, a big Chow from a house on the middle of the block sometimes chased me to the corner. One of my grandmother's old lady friends had a little Pekinese that forever barked at me and nipped me though he didn't seem to bother anyone else. And one afternoon when I was on the school swings with some other kids, a big Collie seemed to come from nowhere, jumped up and grabbed my shoulder with his teeth and pulled me to the ground, and even if he didn't really bite me, he gave me a terrible scare. The girl who owned him said he'd never acted like that before—she couldn't figure it out.

Some of my friends talked about dogs getting rabies, too, and how people could die from the bite of a mad dog. I did see a dog who was foaming at the mouth once, and even if he was in a fenced-in yard I ran all the way home. When I thought about it, if dogs could be so mean and dangerous, then maybe it wasn't such a good idea to want one for a pet. In my experience, dogs like Lad only existed in books, or maybe on the radio, like Sergeant Preston's Yukon King. Like so many other things, I guessed I'd just have to wait till I got older.

Mrs. Mullen, the rent-collector's wife, had a canary in a cage but birds didn't really interest me. Besides, they seemed like the kind of pets for girls. Every once in awhile, someone would bring me a goldfish for the bowl on my dresser, but they never lived very long, even if I did remember to feed them every day. Once I even flushed one down the toilet to set it free. I imagined it swimming though the underground pipes all the way to the Mississippi. After that, my mother said we wouldn't be getting any more goldfish. Maybe a little turtle with a painted shell, the kind they sold at Woolworth's, but to me, turtles were about as interesting as rocks. At least none of the kids I knew in the neighborhood had pets, though Buck Weiskopf said he had a horse that he kept at his grandparents' farm, though I didn't really believe him.

Just be patient, my mother said. Maybe we could get a dog or cat if we ever moved into a house of our own. Then she'd tell me about a dog she used to have named Feller, who was part coyote. That was when she and my father lived in Montana, back before I was born, and she used to ride horses, too—I'd even seen some pictures of her on a horse. She'd get a little teary when she talked about those days before they had to live in the city, but when I asked her if she wanted to move back to Montana she said no, of course not, because now she had me and my sister, which was a lot better. Thinking about how happy she looked in those pictures, I found that a little hard to believe, but the more I thought about it, the more I knew I should stop talking about having a pet, at least around my mother.

Test Pattern

Up until Junior High, the biggest surprise of my life was the day my father brought home a combination radio, record player and TV set. All I'd been hearing about was how we couldn't afford things, and even if the TV screen measured only 7 inches, I knew that console cost a lot more money than anything else we had—though I never did hear any kind of explanation for it.

It was just as surprising how fast the word got out. Even if there were only a couple of programs on in the evenings (except for test pattern, which I sometimes watched anyway), people kept showing up to watch with us— friends of my parents, neighbors, relatives we hadn't seen in awhile, and even a few kids from my class at school, especially the ones I didn't know very well, like Clyde, who'd had surgery for a hare lip and was hard to understand and hard to look at because his nose was always dripping into his mouth. By 7:00 our little livingroom was full of people. It's amazing, everyone would keep saying, and no one would move except my father, who'd occasionally get up to adjust the rabbit ears. A lot of times people would bring some soda pop or ice cream with them, and once in awhile my father even popped some corn on the stove.

All in all, those evenings didn't last very long, as other people started getting TV sets, too, with bigger screens and better reception. Pretty soon it was just our family again in front of the TV set in the evenings, and once in awhile, Clyde, who'd taken to walking up and down the streets at night looking for that TV screen glow in windows, though we were about the only people who'd let him in. I never really understood why my parents would do that, any more than I could understand why my father got the TV set in the first place. But I had to admit, I did enjoy all the attention, even if it was only for a little while.

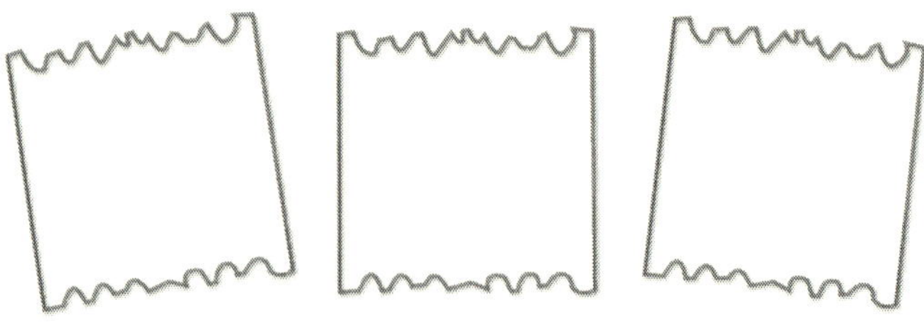

Along for the Ride

Once in awhile my father had to make a day trip for his job and sometimes he'd take me with him, probably because my mother needed some time by herself. Even if we couldn't find a lot to say to each other, sitting in front with my father was a lot better than sitting in the back with my little sister on family trips.

The highways we traveled had only two lanes, and all of them went through a lot of towns, so I did have plenty to look at, and sometimes my father would tell me what crops were growing in the fields we drove by, or about a particularly good café in one of those towns. Sometimes we'd pass other cars, too, staying behind them for what seemed like a long time, easing out and then back until my father was sure it was safe to make his move. He always honked his horn as we went past and the other drivers would usually wave or at least nod. When it got dark, he'd flick the headlights instead of honking.

Day or night we got passed a lot more than we passed anyone else. Everything my father did seemed too slow and too safe—not like my grandfather, who liked to drive 80 in his big Oldsmobile, or my great uncle Minnie, my grandmother's brother, who drove on the highway the same way he did in his farm fields, my grandmother said, and sometimes ended up in the ditch. What I wanted more than anything was to drive fast enough to pass every other car on the highway, to hang my head out the window and scream and wave into the wind.

You'll get where you're going a lot faster if you're steady and take your time, my father would say, puffing on his cigarette until the smoke made my eyes water. Usually he put it out in the ashtray just below the radio, which he wouldn't turn on till it was time for the news, but sometimes, especially at night, he'd let me turn the dial to find some music I liked, and he'd roll down the window to flick his cigarettes out so I could turn and watch the flare of sparks disappearing into the darkness behind us.

Vocational Education

In the small town where she lived, my grandmother knew a woman who was a phrenologist—one of those people who can tell your fortune by putting their hands on your head and reading all the bumps and curves, like a gypsy is supposed to be able to read your palm. I was pretty small when Grandma took me to see this woman, who felt all over my head and then announced I was going to be a preacher when I grew up. That really pleased my grandmother, which was okay with me. I didn't have any idea what a preacher was.

When I got older and sometimes had to go to Sunday church services with my parents, I found out a lot about preachers. The one in our church scared me with all his threats about what would happen to sinful people. There was a much nicer preacher who lived a few houses down the street from us and whose daughter was in my class at school. She was the one who always told the boys what they did was sinful, like swearing or making fun of teachers behind their backs. That girl had three sisters, every bit as holy as she was. I could only imagine what it would be like to grow up in a house like theirs, even though their father and mother never talked like that. The girl also told me that a preacher's family was always poor, because preachers didn't make much money, but that didn't matter because God would always provide.

It was times like those when I'd remember my grandmother's friend and what she predicted, and I'd wonder if all the bumps I'd gotten on my head in the past few years would make any difference. Maybe there was still time to make sure nobody would ever be able to figure out my head.

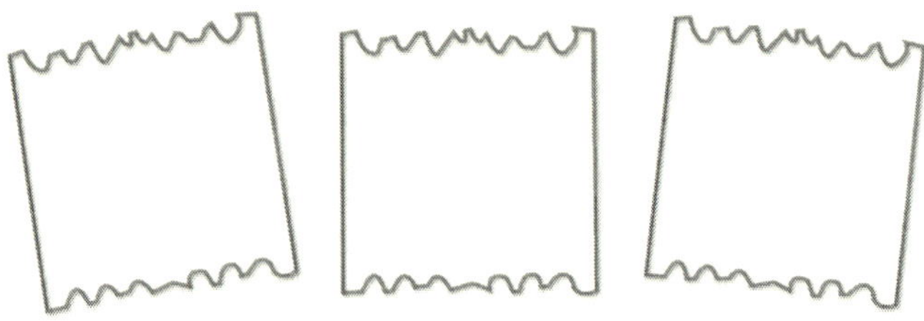

Vocational Education, II

When I was in fourth grade, the classroom job I wanted the most was to be paper monitor, maybe it was because it involved such an nice combination of power and responsibility—enough to earn me the teacher's nodding approval for a change. Or maybe it was because it would make my mother proud when I raced home after school to tell her, especially because she used to be a teacher herself. "I knew you could do it," she'd say, just as she always did.

Being paper monitor meant organizing and passing out whatever papers we needed for the day's schoolwork and then, later, collecting whatever we'd been drawing on or writing on as part of our assignments, and finally stacking all the papers neatly on the table by the teacher's desk, sorting them in the order of the rows our desks were in.

If I was amazed when the teacher chose me for the job, most of my classmates barely seemed to notice, probably because half our class were monitors. There were hall monitors, to make sure we didn't run on the way to or from lunch or recess. There were drinking fountain monitors to make sure no one got pushed or no one butted in when we were lining up. There were coatroom monitors to be sure everything got hung up neatly, and there was even a monitor of monitors—someone to be sure all the other monitors did their jobs.

Most of the monitors, of course, were girls. The teacher made it clear that in *her* experience girls were far more responsible than boys, at least in most positions— especially the ones that involved keeping order. A lot of us boys thought it had more to do with being willing to rat on your classmates. And that, as it turned out, was exactly what happened to me.

Near the end of school on the first day of my new job, Rita, the girl who was the head monitor and also captain of the row I sat in, complained to the teacher that some of the students didn't get all the papers I was supposed to be passing out, and that the papers I had managed to collect simply weren't in the proper order. Some of them were even upside down or backwards. And soon enough, the look on Teacher's face told me that my career as a paper monitor had come to an abrupt end. It also told me to look forward to yet another version of her *hopeless daydreamer* speech.

By the end of the afternoon, I was back at my old job of clapping erasers, sneezing and wheezing in clouds chalk dust. At least I got to go outside for a few minutes, and sometimes with Clyde to help me, though he liked to clap the erasers against his shirt and pants and come back into the classroom looking like some kind of zombie.

Once in awhile I found myself imagining working with people like Clyde when I grew up—the sort of guys I'd seen standing around on loading docks on the way downtown. At least there wouldn't be any girls like Rita there. I was pretty sure that most of them were going to grow up to be teachers.

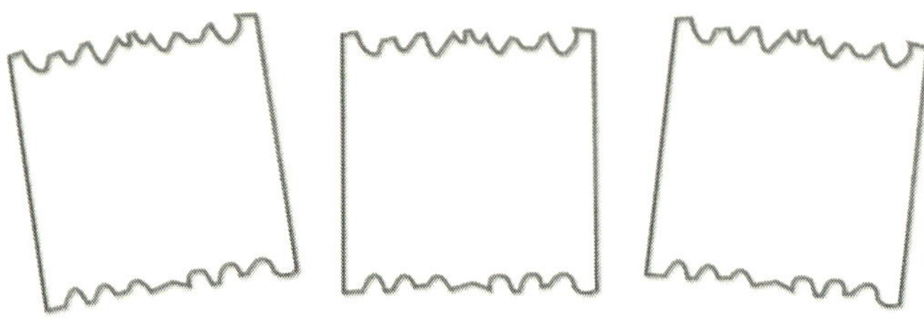

Behind the Lines

Bobby Zappa was the smallest and quietest kid in our class—nobody ever seemed to pay him much attention. But the day our class was making Christmas decorations for our room, the teacher assigned the two of us to be partners. Once we started talking, we found out we got along pretty well together. He had this neat set of little painted metal soldiers, and he always kept a couple of them in his pocket or his desk, which he played with when the teacher couldn't see him—his head ducked down and his eyes darting around like he was on a secret mission or something.

After school one day Bobby said I should come over to his place and see the whole set of soldiers, so we walked together to a small gray house near the railroad tracks. I knew it was much too far to go without letting my mother know first, but I didn't really think about that till we were in Bobby's room, which had cardboard taped over the window. When I asked Bobby about what happened he said it was because his father got so angry sometimes he'd break things, like window glass or dishes or even furniture. Then he showed me the place where his father had nearly put his fist through the closet door.

Just about the time were spreading the soldiers out on the floor, I noticed Bobby's father standing in the doorway, staring down at us like we'd been doing something wrong—not saying a word but kind of snarling. He looked a lot like Bobby, seeming to be half-crouched even when he was standing straight, but it was his eyes that really bothered me. Under his breath, Bobby said I'd better get going, though I wondered how I could, with his father blocking the doorway. He didn't move an inch until I almost bumped into him, and then I found myself squeezing myself out the door and down the back stairs and running as fast as I could go. I couldn't stop thinking about my mother at home waiting for me, and how terrible I felt about making her worry so much all the time, and my father, too, who I'd never seen break anything.

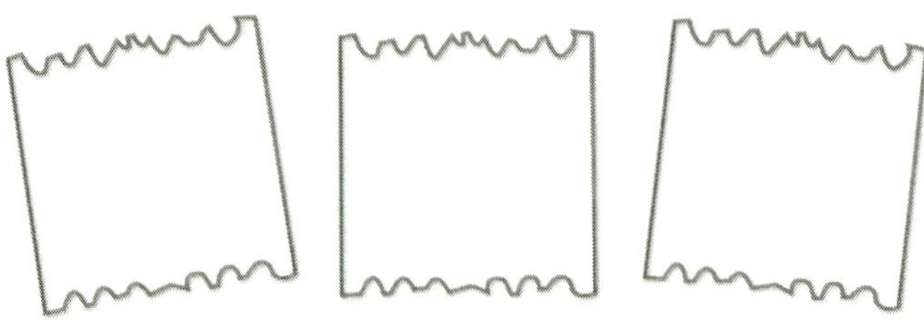

Out of the Woods

Any kid growing up in Minnesota has to listen to stories about the danger of wood ticks and poison ivy each spring, and it was times like those I was glad I lived safely in the middle of Minneapolis. But then, one February day when I was in fourth grade, my mother discovered a wood tick burrowed into the back of my neck, just above the hairline, and starting to swell up with my blood.

The daughter of a doctor, my mother understood the danger of infection that comes from pulling the tick out but leaving the pincers in, so she sent me to school with a note for the nurse, would know the right thing to do. The problem was, the nurse wasn't there that day, so the principal called my father at work and asked him to pick me up and take me to another school, which did have a nurse on duty. He wasn't very happy about that, but at least he wouldn't have to pay for a doctor. Neither he nor the principal wanted to take any chances with the tick, beyond dousing it with rubbing alcohol, which didn't do any good at all.

When my father finally delivered me to the other school, the nurse turned out to be as grouchy as he was. She simply snorted, sat me down on a stool, grabbed the tick with her thumb and forefinger and ripped it out, along with a clump of my hair. "That should do it," was all she said, after applying a lot of disinfectant. When I got home from school, my mother checked my neck carefully and seemed surprised she couldn't find anything wrong.

No one ever did figure out where that tick came from. All my father said when he got home from work was that I wasn't looking any the worse for wear. Maybe he saw my relief that *this* time when something bad happened, it wasn't my fault.

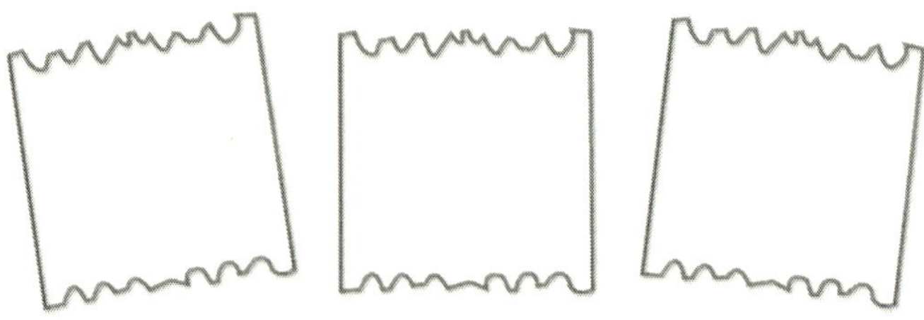

The Most Important Meal

When my father was home, my parents liked to have bacon and eggs for breakfast. When he was gone, which was most of the time, I usually had cold cereal. My mother had such a hard time getting me out of bed and ready for school, there usually wasn't time for anything else. She kept trying to get me to eat oatmeal, doctoring it up, as she called it, with milk and sugar, but it still tasted awful. Even if breakfast was the most important meal of the day, as we kept hearing in school, I'd rather go without anything than eat oatmeal.

In fourth grade when we were studying nutrition, we had to keep a record of every breakfast for three weeks. At first I tried to be truthful about breakfasts but when there got to be too many days with just Wheaties or Cheerios I'd start adding sliced bananas or strawberries, or maybe some toast and raspberry jam. But why stop there? Some days I wrote down pancakes or scrambled eggs and ham. My teacher—the good substitute, not the crabby old regular one—was pretty impressed when she checked my record. It was all I could do to keep from adding t-bone steak or spaghetti. Maybe that was when I first figured out that teachers could be fooled just like anybody else and if what you told them made them pleased, then it wasn't really the same thing as lying, was it?

What I had forgotten about was parent-teacher conferences, which were held a couple of times a year. "Your teacher and I think you've got a pretty good imagination," was all my mother said. It took me awhile to figure out the teacher had showed her my breakfast record and then I felt worse than if either of them had yelled at me. After awhile, when I thought about it some more, I began to realize I was pretty good at making things up, that this wouldn't be the last time I'd get in trouble for it, and that I probably wasn't ever going to stop.

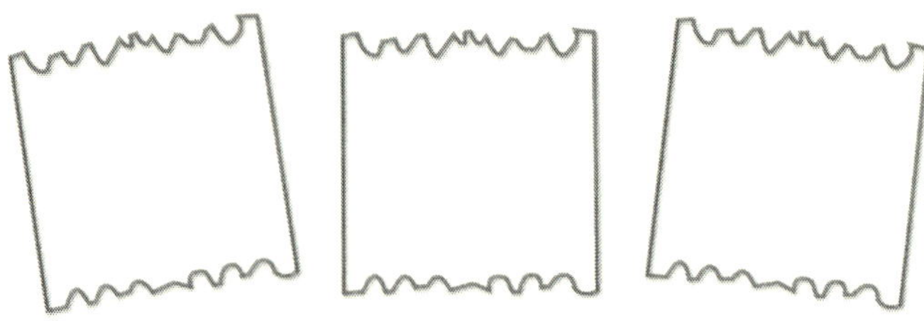

Word of Mouth

Rumors about the fifth grade teacher began to grow not long after we got to fourth grade upstairs. Aside from being very large and old, she supposedly took great pleasure in beating naughty children in the cloakroom that ran between the fourth and fifth grade rooms. We did hear her yelling in there once in awhile, and Bergy told us to listen for a thumping sound on the wall, which was the teacher banging kids' heads against it.

Mostly we had problems enough with our own teacher, who was also very large and old, and strict—not at all like our third grade teacher, who even used to hug us sometimes. Our fourth grade teacher moved two desks beside hers in the front of the room, reserved for talkers or other rule-breakers. I ended up sitting in one of those desks a couple of times—most of the boys did.

The best thing to happen in fourth grade was when our teacher had to have some kind of operation and was gone most of the winter and early spring. We knew things were looking up when the substitute—who ended up staying with us the whole time—moved those two desks back with the others on her very first day with us. The other thing she started right away was a free time period when we got to read whatever we wanted to at our desks, or maybe the whole class would play a game like 20 Questions. The more we grew attached to that always-smiling substitute, the meaner and more threatening the fifth grade teacher next door became. It almost seemed like we'd been given our substitute as a reward for what we were going to have to face the next year.

Just about the time the snow started melting seriously, I came down with a bad cold and had to miss a couple of days of school. The day I returned I could tell immediately that things had changed. That cold, gray silence was back, along with our old teacher, stricter and sterner than ever. It didn't take me long to discover she'd been though my desk. She'd written TAKE THIS HOME AT ONCE on a slip of paper, in reference to the comic book and a couple of toy cars she'd found there. It wasn't long before the two desks were back beside hers in the front of the room.

When we finally made it to the last day of class, our old teacher told us how much she appreciated how good we'd been when she was gone, and that was especially important because we'd be the last class she'd ever teach. She and the fifth grade teacher had decided to retire together and do some traveling. Most of us just sat there stunned at the news. We really didn't understand much about retirement, and while we were relieved about not having to face that scary fifth grade teacher in the fall, we also felt a little cheated, a little disappointed, and we couldn't begin to understand why.

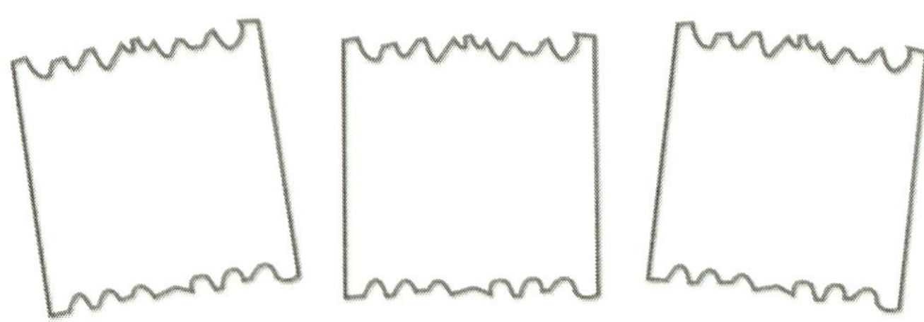

For the Moment

On warm spring evenings most of the people from the apartment houses would take kitchen chairs out on the wooden back balconies and visit with each other, or maybe just sit quietly till it got dark, watching the night hawks swooping and listening to their metallic cries echoing off the buildings.

Spring was the best time of year, before people went away on summer trips or it got too hot to sit outside, even near dark. Once or twice a week the marching band from the Catholic high school would practice in the weedy vacant lot half a block away, the only two songs they seemed to know—*Sweet Violets* and *I'll Be Down to Get You in a Taxi, Honey*—over and over and over again, until all of us knew every note and drumbeat by heart.

Sometimes we could see the beam of a searchlight in the distance and then, if he were in a particularly good mood, my father would get the car out of the garage and he and my mother and little sister and I would drive around till we tracked down the source of that light and then stop for an ice cream cone on the way home.

Sometimes, if there were enough children around, there'd be games of kick-the-can or wagon and bike races around the dirt oval by the garages, but most of the time there was simply the sitting and watching, the quiet voices from behind the porch railings.

And for those moments, no one would be getting sick or dying. There would be no impossible questions to ask or answer, nothing that needed to be done right now. We'd simply be glad of where we were, all of us, as the night hawks dived and the searchlights searched, far above us and forever.

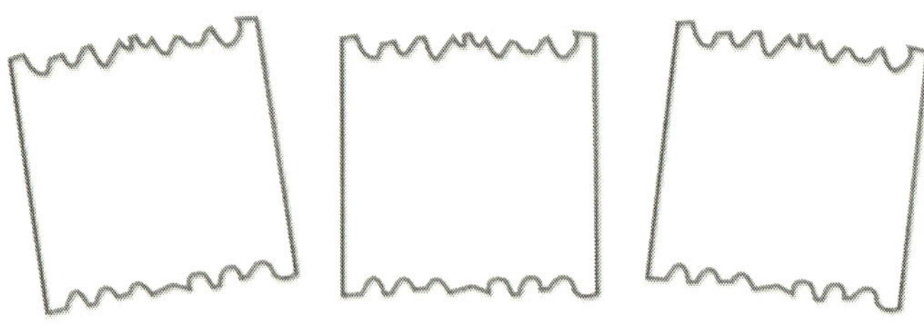

Moving

The summer before fifth grade, we finally got a house like the one my mother had always talked about, but it was in a neighborhood across town. Even so, my parents said it was a place where there were a lot of kids my age and my little sister's age, too. There wouldn't be a lot of old women to run errands for, but there would be a lawn for me to mow and a garden I'd have to help with, and a lot of other new things to get used to. Everything seemed bigger in the new place—the stores and the churches and the school I'd be going to—but when I tried to explain that to Bergy, he just talked about *his* new school, the junior high. I kept saying that he'd have to come and visit me, but he just said he didn't think he'd have time, not with going out for sports and probably finding a girlfriend, and other things I wouldn't understand till I was older.

Bergy's mother said she'd bring him for a visit once we got settled into the new house, but she never did. It was a long time before I stopped missing him and wondering about him. It was a long time, too, before I stopped feeling bad about that big pile of Bergy's comic books that I'd never gotten around to returning, but the day came when it didn't matter anymore and I sold them all to the guy who ran the hobby store for a penny each. I knew he'd turn around and sell them for a nickel but I didn't care. It seemed exactly the sort of thing that Bergy would do himself.

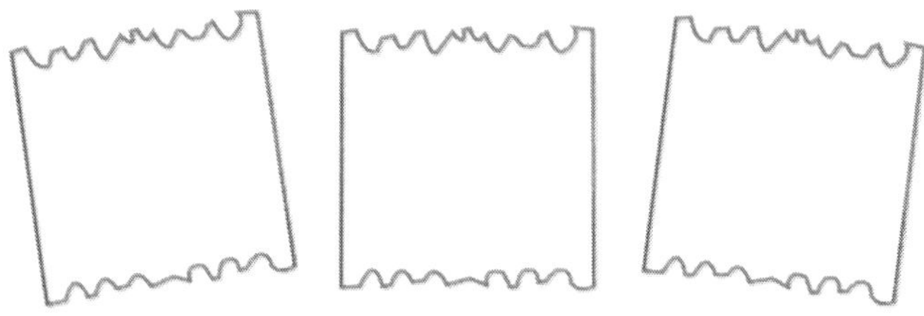

A Place of Our Own

Aunt Molly asked me how I liked having my own yard for a change and she didn't understand when I said I liked the one at the apartment buildings better. She didn't give me a chance to explain that since Bergy and I had the run of the apartment yards, the garages and woodpile and the Catholics' weed field, it was a lot bigger and more interesting than the nice little yard at the new house. Aunt Molly started yelling that I was so ungrateful, that I didn't appreciate how hard my parents had worked so we could have the new house. But I *did* understand that. I could see how happy they were, which is why I'd never say anything to change that.

It was true, too, that the house was pretty neat—a three-bedroom stucco with two stories and a big fireplace in the living room, where my mother promised we could roast marshmallows in the cold weather. There were two apple trees in the back yard, too, one of which was good for climbing and a big basement where my father said we could put up a ping pong table. Even if I still had the smallest bedroom it had neat wallpaper with Canadian Mounties on horseback.

One thing, there were a lot more kids in the new neighborhood—a lot of girls the same age as my little sister, though most of the boys were a year younger than me, so they weren't going to be in my room at school. Unless we could get up a ballgame, I didn't see a lot of those boys, either, since they were usually off somewhere on their bikes. I'd never learned to ride a bike because at the old place there wasn't anywhere to keep one in a second floor apartment, and since none of the other kids I knew had bikes either, I hadn't missed having one.

For the first time I could remember, I was ready for school to start, so I'd have the chance to meet some new boys in my class. When I told my father the part about school starting, he looked as surprised as I'd ever seen him look. Living in a new house was turning out to be a lot more complicated than any of us had ever expected.

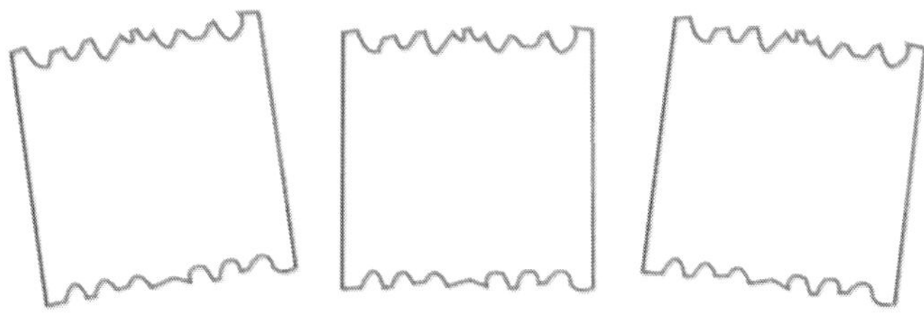

Odd Jobs

The old woman who lived next door, on the corner, came over one day and asked if I'd be available to do some odd jobs around her house, like painting the basement stairway. That was really an odd job since I'd never painted anything before, but I'd seen my father do it and it didn't look too hard. Anyway, I must have done a good enough job because after that she asked me to do some other things, like getting up on a stepladder to clean the gutters around her house, which I was glad was only one-story. Her husband, who looked like he was much too old to still be working, drove off to his office every day, even Saturdays, though he did mow his lawn with a noisy old power mower on Sundays, right about the time we'd be eating Sunday dinner. My father said it was just his luck to live next door to the only noisy mower in the neighborhood. On the other hand, My father seemed pretty pleased that I was taking some responsibility, as he called it. And if I could paint for the neighbors, then I could certainly do it at home—like all those storm windows stacked up in the garage. As soon as I asked him how much I was going to get paid for the job, I knew it was a mistake. "You live here, don't you?" he said.

After that, our neighbor pretty much ran out of odd jobs for me to do, though my father did raise my allowance eventually. But then, I had a lot of things to do, like mow the grass and help pick stuff in the garden and vacuum the carpeting on the stairs once a week. It seemed my parents dreamed up a new job for me nearly every day, though they kept themselves pretty busy too. The hardest part about living in the new place was knowing that every time my father was working around the house or yard, he expected me to be working too.

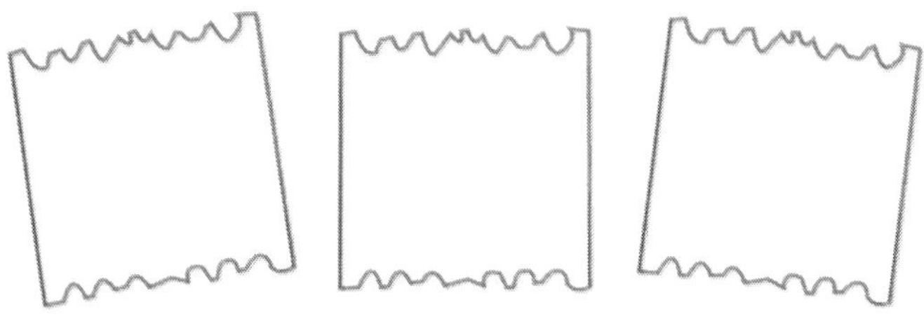

Family Still Life

Every evening when he came home from work, my father would take off his coat and tie and sit at the kitchen table with the evening paper and a bottle of beer. When I was in thirrd or fourth grade he gave me a sip from his glass and when I said I liked it pretty well, he poured a little more beer in a shot glass just for me—and did that whenever I'd sit with him at the table after he came home. He never said much those times, and not during meals either. When my mother would ask him how he liked what she'd fixed for dinner, he'd say he was eating it, wasn't he?

What I didn't understand till later was that my father was partially deaf and he hated to wear his hearing aid at home. Sometimes at the table when I'd be talking to my mother about something that had happened at school or in the neighborhood, my father would get angry because he thought we were talking about him. Other times, when I *was* talking about him, my father could hear every word and then I'd get into trouble. There was no predicting when he could or couldn't hear me, which was another of the things that made it hard to be around him, though it did, as he said, teach me to keep on my toes—in that department I seemed to need all the practice I could get.

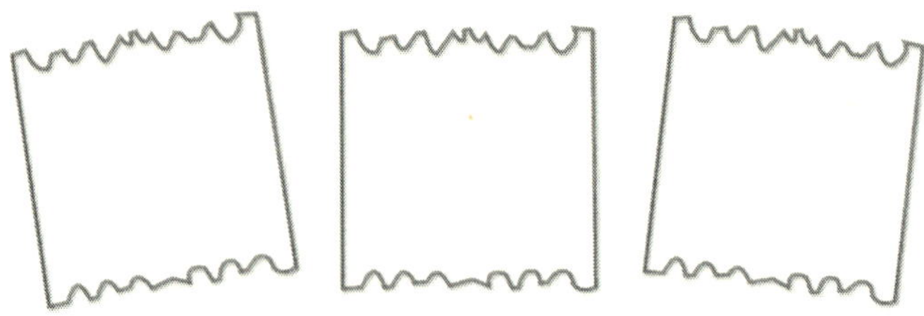

A-Hunting We Will Go

Sometimes in the fall when my father went on trips for his job he'd take his shotgun with him in the car, maybe to visit some friends along the way who happened to have a duck blind, or maybe just to stop somewhere in the country and walk the edges of a field by himself to scare up some grouse or pheasants. Then, when he'd get home and I'd go down to help him bring stuff inside, I might find that I had a couple of ducks to carry by their long necks and impress whoever might be sitting on the back balcony, especially Bergy, whose father didn't even own a shotgun. I had to wonder if I was going to be much of a hunter when I grew up, because it was all I could do to carry those birds up the stairs without getting sick to my stomach. At least my father waited till I was in bed to clean his game in the kitchen sink, though sometimes I'd see their heads in the pail of garbage it was my job to haul downstairs to the big cans by the garages. I never really liked the taste of wild game, either, when my father would roast a bird for Sunday dinner, though I'd always try to eat a little and make him happy.

When I got a little older, and after we'd moved to our new house, he took me hunting one time, just the two of us. We prowled along this dirt road beside a woods looking for grouse, though we never saw any. Then, when it was about time to leave, my father decided it was a good place for me to learn how to shoot his .12 gauge shotgun. He laid the barrel on top of a strand of a barbed wire fence and helped me aim at a rusty gallon gas can a few yards away, but he didn't tell me to hold the gun's stock tight against my shoulder, so when I finally pulled the trigger the gun was about a couple of inches from my shoulder and the kick knocked me over backwards. My father just smiled when he helped me up and said that would be enough for today and next time I'd do a lot better. My shoulder stayed sore for three or four days, with this incredible bruise I'd keep checking in the mirror. At least I'd be able to tell my friends I'd shot a real gun, though every time I saw that bruise I'd seem to be reminded how different my life was going to be from my father's.

The Chosen

Bergy never let me forget that he was two years older and got chosen to be a Safety Patrol in sixth grade. That's something I had wanted to do for a long time. When I was younger I'd even made a little flag out of a bandana tied to a long stick, the kind the Safety Patrols held up to stop traffic when they stepped out into the street wearing their white cross-belts. Maybe it was because the smaller kids depended so much on the Patrols, or maybe it was the special picnic they all got to go to around the time school let out for the summer, I couldn't think of anything I'd rather be than a Patrol. I hated to see Bergy out there on the corner making me stop whenever he pleased or bragging about how great it was to get out of class early every day so he could get out to his post. Since a fourth-grader couldn't be a Patrol, I knew I'd just have to keep my mouth shut and wait at least another year to get picked, but that didn't stop me from imagining being one.

When I started fifth grade in the new school, the Patrols had already been chosen by the teachers, and since it was a much bigger school, I guessed I probably wouldn't ever get chosen. One good thing—all the Patrols were stationed on the other side of the school from the one where I walked home and there weren't any busy streets to cross. Even if I had to see them leave the classroom every day when the teacher called "Patrols, it's time," at least I didn't have to watch them doing their jobs, having all that fun.

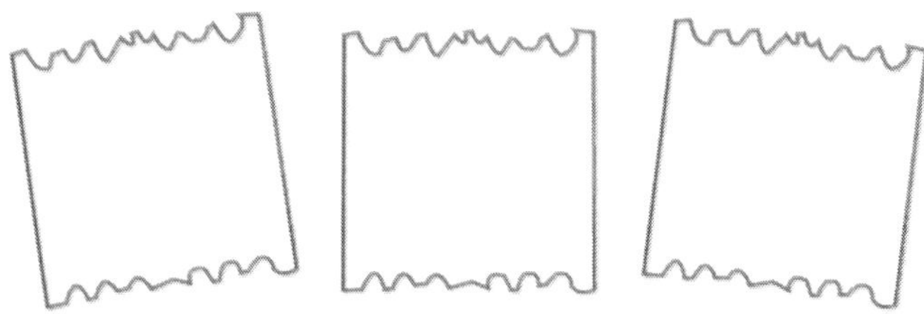

The Daredevil

In our fifth grade class, Charlie was the kid who always smeared his ink and erased holes in his paper, who usually forgot his homework and tracked in mud from the school yard and got sent back to clean his shoes three or four times till he got it right. Charlie was the only kid I ever knew who dared to let farts during the flag salute, who put tacks on the teacher's chair even though she always checked before she sat down. Charlie was the one who told me my first really filthy joke. In fact, he told the whole class, one day when our teacher decided we should try something called Joke Sharing Time, which thanks to Charlie lasted only about five minutes and was never held again, not even on the best of days.

I had to wonder how much Charlie really liked being alone all the time. Maybe he got used to everybody laughing at him, or maybe he just didn't care. One thing was for certain—we all counted on Charlie to take the pressure off the rest of us. We really didn't understand that till he moved away near the end of sixth grade and there was suddenly this big hole in our classroom. "You guys don't know what you're missing" was Charlie's favorite expression, whether he was sliding into base head first on a gravel playground or on his way to the principal's office. We were finally realizing how right he was.

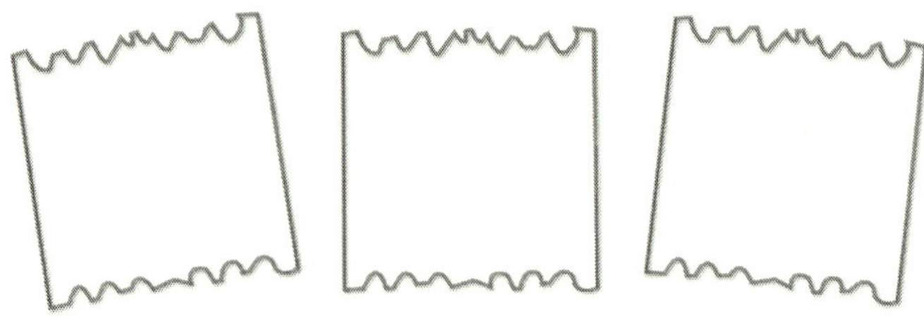

A Poor Excuse

Some of my favorite times were when I was sick enough to stay home from school but not sick enough so I couldn't enjoy myself. Listening to the radio in my room and eating saltines with ginger ale was a lot better than most days at school, especially after we moved. One time in fifth grade I had a book report due and hadn't even started reading the book, so I got the idea of packing my nose with pepper till I really began sneezing and my nose stayed red and runny—enough to convince my mother I was really sick. By lunch time I started to think I was smart enough to pretty much stay home from school any time I wanted to, until my mother came to my room a bowl of soup and discovered what she called my remarkable recovery. After she'd taken my temperature and found it was normal, she reminded me that her father was a doctor and she'd spent a lot of time helping him out in his office, even when she was my age. And then she said I'd better get done whatever it was that needed getting done because I certainly wasn't going to stay home another day.

Even though I had most of the rest of the day to read that book for my report I just couldn't bring myself to do it for some reason. Then, when I had to give my report to the class the next day I mainly repeated what was written about the book on the back cover, and after school the teacher called me in and said how disappointed she was. I was surprised how much she looked like my mother when she said that—a little angry and a little sad. I wished to myself that someday soon I'd really be sick—but not too sick—so my teacher and my mother would both be nice to me when I really deserved it.

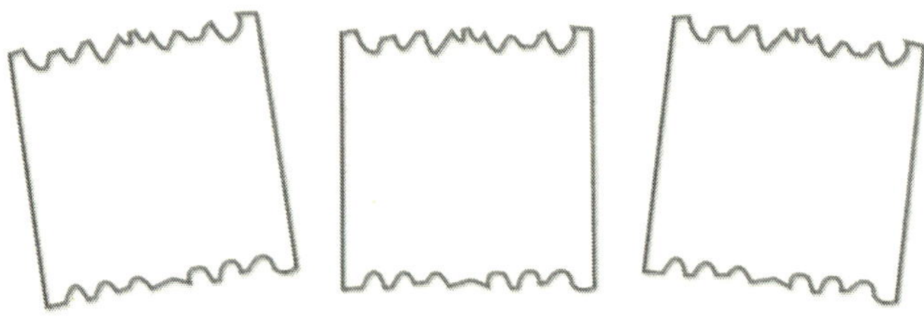

Our Gang

Since some of the people in the apartment house where we lived did a lot of canning in the summer, my friends and I found an almost endless supply of wooden fruit crates in the junk pile out behind the garages. Most Saturday mornings would find us with our fathers' hammers and nails and saws, trying to knock together some kind of inspired contraption, just like the kids in the *Our Gang* comedies did. All we ever came up with was another pile of junk, along with a lot of bent nails and bruised fingers.

When I got a little older, those short films were called *The Little Rascals* and we watched them on TV nearly every day after school. By then we'd stopped trying to build our own race cars or fire trucks, but the way that group of kids always stuck up for each other inspired us to form our own sort of club, though we never found very much to hold us together. We didn't have bullies or snotty rich kids to outsmart, and none of us had a mule or a monkey, or even a mangy dog like Petey—only a couple of pathetic turtles and goldfish.

My mother used to watch with us once in awhile and liked to remind us that when some of those movies were made, she wasn't that much older than kids like Spanky and Darla were, and that she'd even had a black friend named Buster, who reminded her a lot of Stymie. But she'd grown up in a small town, which seemed a much better place for a bunch of kids to hang out together and build stuff and have adventures than in the big city neighborhood where we lived. Besides, it was too hard to imagine my mother being the same age as those kids on TV. "Just you wait," she'd tease us. "Some day you'll be watching those Rascals with your own kids." That's when we'd fall down on the floor laughing. "Sure," we said. "That'll be the day!"

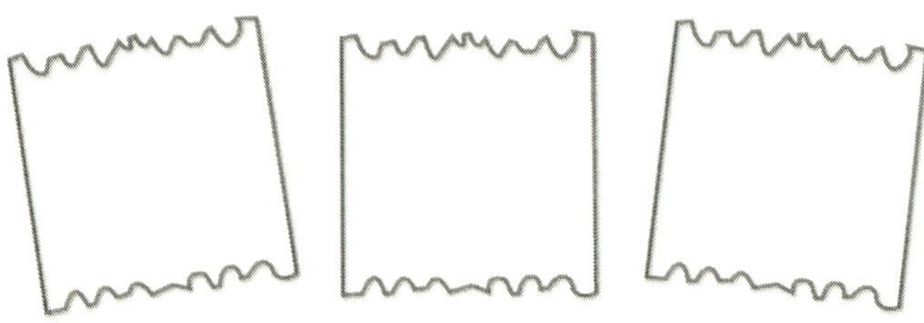

Dodge Ball

When I started fifth grade in my new school there was a game that everyone in my classroom had played but me, and the first time I played it I kept getting stuck in the middle of the circle, where I got hit with the ball so many times that even some of the girls made fun of me for being so slow. It took me a long time to get to like Dodge Ball—learning to aim better and throw harder and harder, especially so I could hit some of those girls.

Mostly that fall the boys played softball and the girls jumped rope or just stood around talking, but when we had to have gym class it was just about always Dodge Ball, which always seemed to involve making fun of people and often ended up with somebody crying. I couldn't understand how our teacher could let something like that happen week after week, especially with the boys and girls together, which made it just about impossible not to be embarrassed. I started to have dreams of that circle of kids throwing the ball at the one caught in the middle, harder and harder as the circle tightened. All of us were learning the only hits that count are the ones that you can really feel, the ones that last.

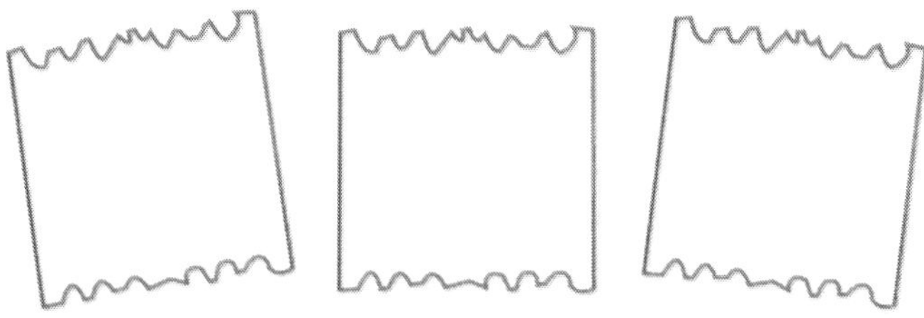

Red Rover

The only advantage of being the tallest and heaviest kid in my classroom came on those days we played red Rover at recess. It was then that the teacher divided us into two teams stretched out into facing lines maybe 50 feet apart, which took turns calling out the names of the kids they wanted to test their lines: "Red Rover, Red Rover, send so-and-so right over!" We all knew that no matter how fast they could run, the skinny girls didn't have much of a chance of breaking through the line of linked arms, but teacher made sure every name got called at least once. When it was my turn, everyone expected me to break through, which I always did—until one day, for no apparent reason, the other side actually stopped me, held me, threw me back as they laughed and cheered. Maybe it was then, as sudden as the autumn downpour that chased us back to our classroom, I understood there were no rules that couldn't be broken, that I was simply fat, not strong, not husky, as my father sometimes called me, and not some budding football star. Maybe it was then I knew my only hope for the future was as unpredictable as the bad weather that would keep us indoors at our desks.

The Star

"Under the leaf sat a warty toad" was the way it was written in our reading books, but when it was Weird Charlie's turn to read aloud it became "under the leaf sat a watery turd." When he said that, the teacher got really red in the face and told him to go and stand outside the classroom door and think about what he had said, but Charlie stood by his desk instead and stared right back at the teacher. Then he turned and announced to the whole class that he liked it a lot better *his* way. That was when the teacher moved quicker than any of us could have thought possible and marched Charlie out of the classroom and down to see the principle, Mrs. Jasperson—Mrs. Gas Bag, as Charlie called her. None of us were surprised that he didn't come back till just before school got out at 3:15.

It also didn't surprise us that Charlie would never admit to anyone that he'd done anything wrong. After school the next few days when the boys divided up into softball teams, Charlie got picked ahead of everybody for the first—and probably the only—time in his life.

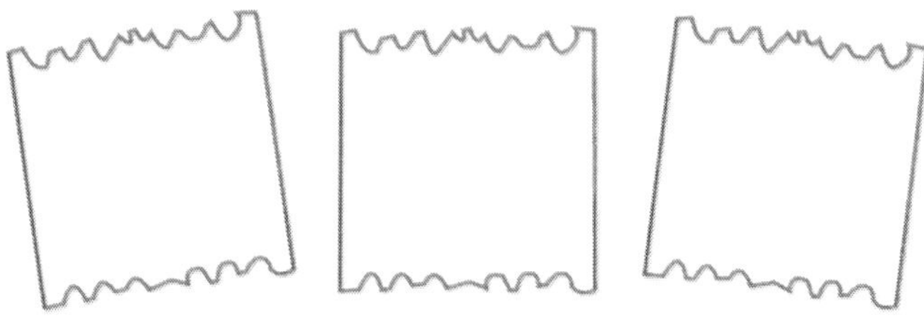

The Grasshopper

Once we moved to our house, I had to start helping my father with a lot of things, like putting up storm windows. Since I was afraid to climb the long, shaky ladder, and not strong enough to slide the heavy windows up to him, my job was to wash them with soapy water from a bucket, spray them with the hose and wipe them down—but there were always streaks, no matter how careful l was, no matter how much time I took.

That first fall, it stayed too hot to be putting up storm windows, but we had to do it because my father was going to be gone on a long trip. Even before the leaves started turning yellow, there were storm windows leaning against the side of the house and the apple tree. "Do them over if you can't get the streaks out," my father kept saying, taking off his sweat-soaked shirt. I knew I'd never have muscles like his. I knew too that I'd never be able to climb that ladder—not the way he could, like the trapeze man I saw at the circus once. "Hurry up," came the voice from the top of the ladder. "Winter will be here a lot sooner than you think!" That made me remember the story about the grasshopper and the ants, and I suddenly imagined that my family, all of them, were ants and I was just a hopeless grasshopper and would always be one. "Hurry up," came the voice from the top of the ladder. "Haven't you noticed how late it's getting?"

The Uncrackable Code

In the winter of fifth grade some of the girls in our room at school decided to form a club with a name made up of the first initials of all of their names, and because of that, some of us boys formed our own club, which didn't have a name because we never could agree on one. Our main purpose was to intercept the notes the girls' club passed back and forth in the classroom and to ambush them with snowballs after school. The notes we managed to steal from their desks were written in code, and even though we spent a lot of time trying to figure it out, we never could crack it. We did find out that the girls were having slumber parties at each others' houses and eventually they even started to dress alike. That was when the boys in our club began to lose interest, or maybe it was the early spring weather and the chance to play softball again.

Whatever it was, by the time sixth grade rolled around in the fall, everyone seemed to have forgotten about clubs. Some of the boys even started walking girls home after school. The only thing that remained from the year before was the secret code the girls still used for notes to each other. It substituted numbers and letters for other letters and shouldn't have been that hard to solve but it was. I found one of those notes in a wastebasket and spent a lot of time trying to figure it out before I gave up. But then, even if I had cracked that code, I realized that probably no one would have cared anymore.

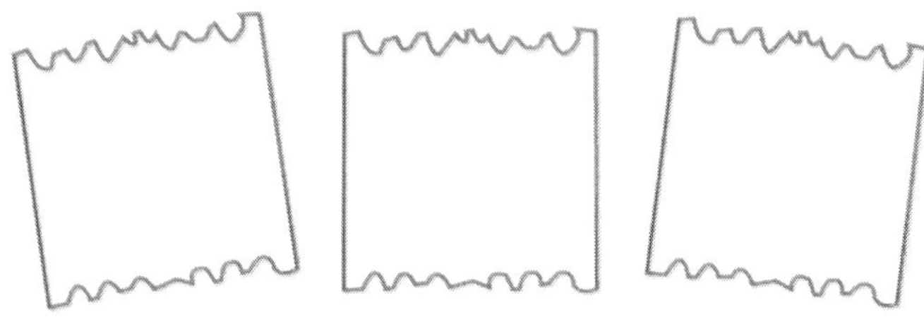

Dumb Luck

The worst thing about going to the doctor's office for a checkup was getting a shot, which happened just about every time, and which I'd agonize about for days before the visit. Since my mother's father had been a doctor, she was especially good about making appointments, downtown in the Medical Arts Building where our doctor had a big office. And while going downtown with my mother would usually mean an interesting bus ride and lunch downtown afterwards, I couldn't stop myself from thinking how much that shot was going to hurt and scare me, even if my mother kept saying it'd be over before I knew it and I was a big boy who shouldn't cry. But I did cry, and beg, and promise just about anything if I didn't have to face that needle.

Going to the doctor was a lot like going to the dentist, and in the same building too. His needle had novacain and hurt even more than the doctor's, to say nothing to the grinding of the drill. He tried to explain once that it wasn't so bad to be hurt a little to keep from being hurt a lot, but to me, the hurting itself was all that was important, and when I was done at either the doctor's or dentist's office, I'd be almost crazy with happiness because it would be such a long time till my next visit. But then, of course, it wouldn't very long at all before I'd be counting off the last few days all over again.

When we moved to our new house, we changed doctors and dentists too—people my father knew, who probably gave him special rates. The new dentist was the son of a friend and just out of dental school. I only went to him a couple of times but the next dentist I went to told me my teeth were nearly ruined. On the other hand, he said I was really lucky—he could fix the damage in just a few visits.

That was when I started to wonder what being lucky really meant. And if I was relieved that the new doctor didn't give me any shots the first time I visited him, after all the questions he asked, I also had to hope that he didn't want to redo anything my old doctor had done. I was starting to believe that what being lucky didn't have much to do with not getting hurt but with finding someone who could do things right the first time.

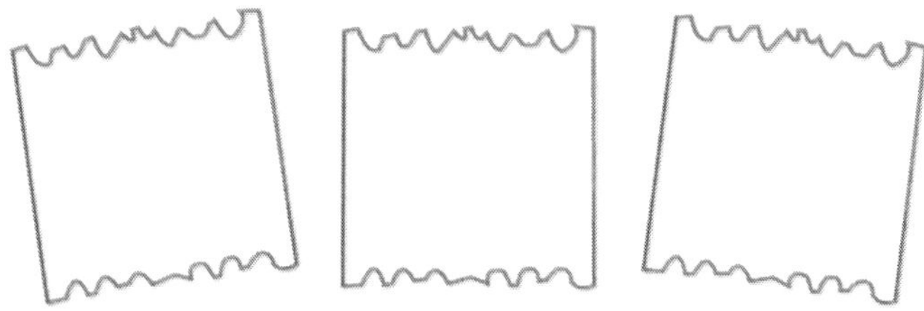

Bath Time

Baths always meant it was time to come in and get ready for bed, a good time to start thinking about tomorrow, my mother said, which I usually didn't want to think about—a good time to examine myself and dream of another body, one that wouldn't betray me.

Grownups never seemed to take so many baths, especially not my grandmother, my father's mother, who warned that they weakened you. I had to love her for that, especially those nights when I got sent back to scour the bathtub ring with Ajax. People kept telling me I'd probably get married one day and have kids of my own, go to work just like my father, buy a car and a house somewhere. Except for the car, it all sounded pretty boring. Washcloth in my pasty, wrinkled fingers, I'd find myself daydreaming about leaving home right then and there and about the things I might do, the places I might go. How much they were going to miss me, all of them—the wonderful boy who used to live here and simply disappeared one day, as if he'd scrubbed himself away and gurgled down the drain.

Guest Appearance

I couldn't believe it when my friend Pete told me that the Lone Ranger was coming to the southside, where I lived. The Lone Ranger was one of my favorites, first from radio and comic books and then from his weekly program on TV, and when I ran home to ask my mother she said yes, she'd read in the paper that the actor who played the Lone ranger would be making what she called a guest appearance at Powderhorn Park, which was a big park that took up several city blocks and even had a small lake in the middle of it. She said that maybe a few of my friends could get together the next Saturday and walk to the park, but that I should also plan to take my little sister, who was only in kindergarten but who had her own Lone Ranger billfold and cowgirl hat.

Much to my relief, it turned out that my sister went with her friend Donna and her mother from next door, so it was just Pete and me and a couple of the other boys from our class at school, but when we got to the park on Saturday afternoon it was already filled with what seemed like thousands of kids, most of them with their parents, and a lot of them wearing Lone ranger masks, sixguns and holsters, hats, boots, and whatever else the Lone Ranger people had been selling. After we all waited about an hour without being able to see much of anything, a roar started to go up from the part of the crowd nearest to the lake, and suddenly there he was, the Lone Ranger on his big white horse, Silver, riding along the far side of the lake—which the police had roped off from the crowd. He kept waving his hat as everybody cheered, and a lot of the kids and even some of the grownups started pushing to get closer to the lake so they could see better. But it didn't really matter because all the lone Ranger did was ride back in forth a couple of times and then he was gone someplace where we couldn't see him any more.

One of the boys from my class at school said he heard a bunch of workers had loaded Silver into a truck and driven off in a big hurry, probably to some other city, some other crowd of kids, and then the Lone Ranger himself had jumped into a big white Cadillac and been driven away, right behind the truck. At first I couldn't believe that a hero like the Lone Ranger would have done that when there were all those kids waiting just to hear him give a little speech or say "Hi-yo Silver" or whatever, but I somehow found it hard not to believe that kid from school. I decided to tell my little sister that there was big trouble in a town not far away and someone had made a special emergency trip to ask the Lone Ranger to come and help, so he really didn't have much of a choice. She thought that was probably okay, even if she didn't get to see him at all because Donna's mother had decided to drive her car and couldn't find a place to park and by the time they went back to her house and walked back to the park, they were at the back of the crowd and couldn't see anything. He was really pretty neat, I told her, but I also said I'd heard he'd be back real soon because he felt so bad about having to leave early, and as much as I hated myself for all those lies it was better than the feeling I got in my stomach whenever I thought of that masked man, whoever he might have been, over on the other side of the lake where we could barely see him, riding back and forth for two for three whole minutes while all of us in the crowd just stood there and cheered like idiots.

Consumer Report

On the way downtown there was a huge billboard with flashing lights for Grain Belt beer. Much to my disappointment, it wasn't the beer my father drank—he could get much better deals on other brands I'd never heard of, and I found it hard to believe him when he said he liked those other brands better than Grain Belt, better even than Hamm's, the beer with the catchy jingle my little sister had learned to sing before she could say a sentence. When I thought about it, I didn't see many things in our house that were advertised on billboards or TV—no Green Giant or Betty Crocker when the A&P store brands were just as good; no Firestone tires or Motorola TV or Maytag washer either.

I always got Buster Brown shoes since the doctor said I needed special support, but a lot of my clothes were marked irregular and came from sales in department store basements. They're every bit as good, my mother tried to convince me. I probably couldn't even find any flaws no matter how hard I looked. "We don't buy clothes to fit your head," my father said—which always made me laugh, remembering the time my little sister danced around the living room, wearing her underpants like a hat. What wasn't funny was those shirts my grandmother sewed for me in colors and patterns she thought were pretty and which I'd fight with my mother about wearing to school, knowing how much I was going to get teased.

When I was old enough to go downtown on the bus with my friend Pete, I shopped around till I found an Arrow shirt on sale and then bought it with some of the money I'd saved from Christmas. It never fit very well and I had to make sure not to wear it when my father was home—not wanting to hear him talk about his son with the well-dressed head.

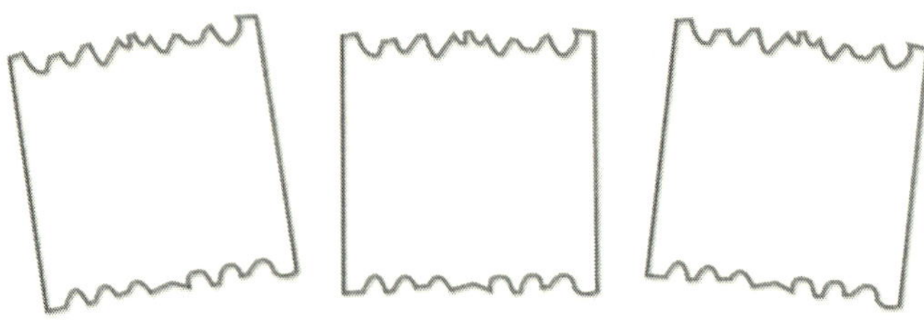

Clipped

My father knew an old barber named Oscar, who had a shop with three other barbers close to the Varsity Theater. I had my instructions—no matter if any of those other barbers wasn't busy, I was to wait for Oscar, which always embarrassed me, especially when I'd have to sit there while barbers with empty chairs kept looking at me. It got so I dreaded going to the barber shop, even if one time a man gave me a quarter to let him go to Oscar ahead of me.

After we moved, I got haircuts from the father of one of my classmates, whose shop was attached to the front of his house and was the only one in our neighborhood. My parents both said that this barber was no Oscar, but since he ran the shop by himself, at least I didn't have to get embarrassed about waiting. I *was* embarrassed whenever my father took me to a friend of his named Tacky who was a barber in the small town where my father grew up, which we sometimes visited in the summer. Maybe it was because this barber was so busy talking to my father or the other customers, but my haircuts were always lopsided, and once he even kept nicking me with the clippers and made both of my ears bleed. My father was always pleased to visit his friend and to save some money on the haircut at the same time, so I never said anything.

My worst haircut came one summer when I was visiting my grandparents and my grandmother decided she was going to cut my hair with the electric clippers she sometimes used to trim my grandfather's hair, though he was pretty bald. She made me sit on a high stool in the kitchen with a dish towel wrapped around my shoulders, and sometimes the clippers seemed to get stuck and start pulling my hair out instead of cutting it. It didn't really surprise me when I ended up looking like one of the farm kids with what people called a white sidewall haircut. I tried not to go outside till my hair grew out, but of course that wasn't possible, and I even forgot about it for awhile, until some of the boys in my grandparents' neighborhood started calling me a little farmer. "Sticks and stones," my grandmother kept reminding me, but I could tell she was laughing a little too.

Summer Saturdays

After we'd been in our new house for a year or so, my father didn't have to travel so much. He especially seemed to enjoy being home on Saturdays, when he and my mother would sit at the kitchen table sorting coupons and then head off to the grocery stores. Sometimes they'd come back with whatever fresh fruit was in season and on sale, like cherries or apricots or peaches, and then they'd spend the rest of the day canning that fruit in the steamy hot kitchen. I remember my father best in an old pair of pants and undershirt, wiping the sweat from his face with a red bandana after hauling a rack of Mason jars from the big canning kettle on the stove, and my mother, the only time I'd ever see her in jeans, cleaning fruit at the sink, pushing her damp hair out of her eyes with the back of a free hand.

My job was to pick the beans and tomatoes from the mosquito-ridden garden, which I hated but which did give me a sense of being part of things, especially on the days when it was beans or tomatoes being canned and I'd get to help. Not much was ever said, but there wasn't a need to say much, all of us together in the kitchen, and my mother at the sink, turning to smile at her men, as she called us, brushing back the damp strands of hair from her eyes.

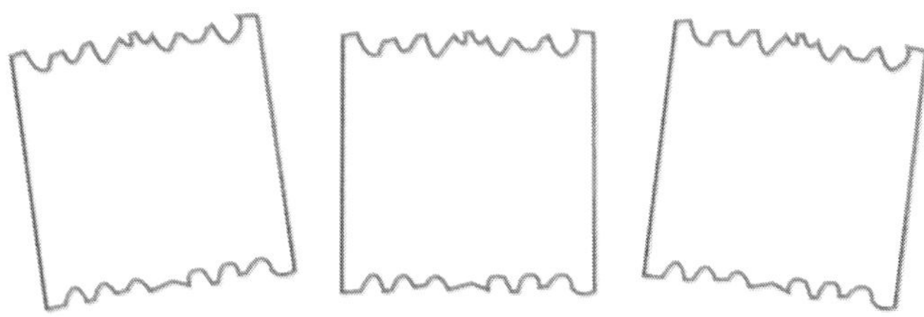

The Sleuth

Even though I was always good at it, I really didn't enjoy reading. Some of my teachers tried to find books they thought I'd really get interested in, like stories about animals or the life story of somebody famous, both of which I thought were really boring. All that began to change when I discovered the Hardy Boys books in sixth grade, and for the next couple of years I read my way through the whole series.

Maybe it was because I liked the world those two brothers lived in, where boys got to do all kinds of neat things and travel to exciting places. Or maybe it was the idea of being a detective, of being clever enough to solve crimes by using your head. The closest I'd ever come to that was during games of Clue on my grandmother's front porch in the summers.

I kept looking for some kind of mystery to solve in my own neighborhood, besides helping my mother remember where she'd put her thimble or her pen. There just wasn't anything to get excited about, except, of course, the reading itself, and talking those books over with my friend Pete, who'd become hooked on the Hardy Boys too. We couldn't wait to find a new book in the series and then share it. We even gave Hardy Boy books to each other as Christmas presents, though of course we'd read them ourselves irst.

When I really thought about it, maybe it wasn't so bad I didn't have crimes to investigate, which also meant that I lived in a good neighborhood. And to my parents, anyway, the fact I'd become so interested in reading meant I'd finally solved one of the biggest mysteries of all.

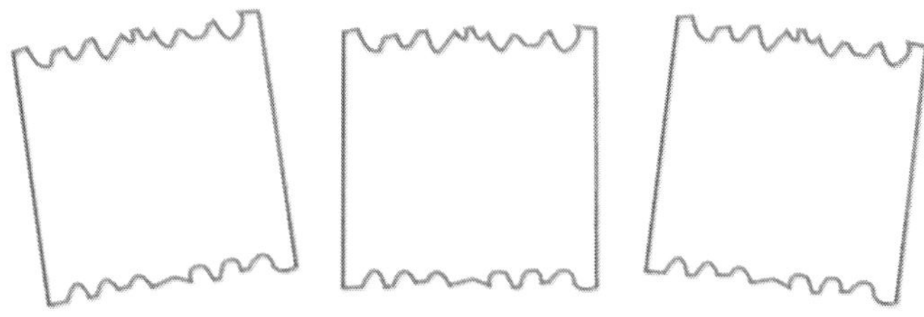

Good Scout

At first I thought being a Cub Scout was pretty neat, especially on the days we got to wear our Scout shirts and neckerchiefs to school, but it was also a lot harder to earn those merit badges than I'd ever imagined, and it got to the point that wearing that shirt was just another way of showing what I hadn't accomplished.

I don't know what I expected, but most of our Den meetings seemed to involve horsing around or maybe shooting baskets and then having milk and cookies. The best meeting I remember was when we were telling jokes and I made Dennis Larson blow milk through his nose when I told a particularly good one. Our problem definitely seemed to be the fact that we never got organized. At our Pack meetings there'd be these older guys leading group sings or showing slides about canoeing or pitching tents, but by the time we were supposed to start thinking about becoming Boy Scouts, a couple of kids had moved away and nobody's mom volunteered to take over as Den Mother. That was also about the time of the big Scout jamboree that was held at the city auditorium. It had some pretty interesting exhibits but also this show with some lousy singing and then what seemed like several hundred of us had to take part in a dramatization of Custer's Last Stand. Our Troop was among the painted Indians but nobody ever told us what to do so we just ran around in circles and screamed as loud as we could and then fell down like we'd been shot by the soldiers in their Cub Scout shirts with cap pistols. Not even the free ice cream afterwards made that trip worthwhile.

Not long after the Jamboree, they sent out a Boy Scout Troop leader to talk to three or four of the disorganized Dens in the basement of some church not far from where we lived. Even though he seemed a lot older than my father, he was dressed up in a Scout uniform with shorts, wearing all these bird calls he'd carved, on lanyards around his neck. He told us how much Scouting had meant to him. Being a good Scout, he said, was just about the most important thing there was, and that we should really pay attention to all that stuff in our manuals. Every time I thought about that man in his too-small uniform, it made me sad, though it also made it easier for me to decide I was going to start going to the YMCA instead.

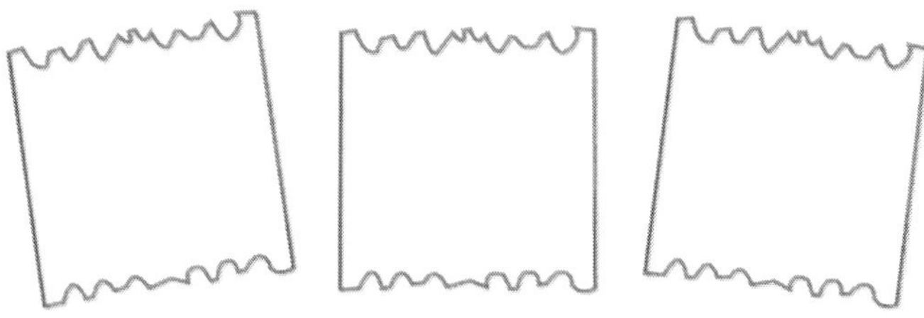

Fairy Tales

"Jack in the Beanstalk" was my favorite fairy tale, maybe because it always gave me hope. Jack was basically a lazy lout—which is what my father sometimes called me when he got angry—but Jack still found a way to become a success. It always came down to taking a risk on those magic beans. Smething for nothing, my father always said. He knew all about boys who squandered everything they got, who had precious little to show for anything.

I had to admit it didn't look good for finding any unusual beans in my neighborhood, and I'd already given up the idea of having been switched at birth by Gypsies. I wasn't clever enough to win any princesses or even to keep from getting lost in the woods, and I certainly didn't have Jack's guts or good luck. Only one thing seemed familiar: the feeling that something huge was smelling my blood, closing in on me, gaining ground each day.

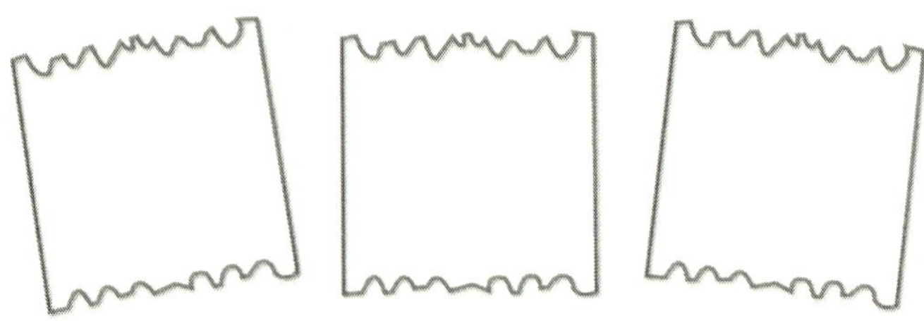

Fireworks

The best thing about being sent to my grandmother's house for a summer visit was that fireworks were legal where she lived. I spent every nickel I could earn or swipe on firecrackers. The other good thing about her town was that it was small enough so that no one paid very much attention to what I and the other boys did—no one but her, that is.

You'll put an eye out, my grandmother said every day. She was certain of it. I hated to disappoint her, but that's what I did best—blowing her jar lids thirty feet in the air, blowing up vegetables from the garden, dolls and toy cars, grasshoppers and garter snakes. "Your cousin lost his finger," Grandma said, but I knew that was from a blasting cap, not a firecracker. My cousin, who was almost as old as my parents, told me he couldn't figure out what it was so he thought he'd take it apart and then it went off and he was sitting there staring at the place his finger used to be.

Sometimes I'd dream about losing an eye or finger, that army of wounded boys who didn't listen to their grandmothers. "Tell me," I could hear Grandma saying, "what are you going to do when you've spent all your money on fireworks? What are you going to do when you've blown everything up?"

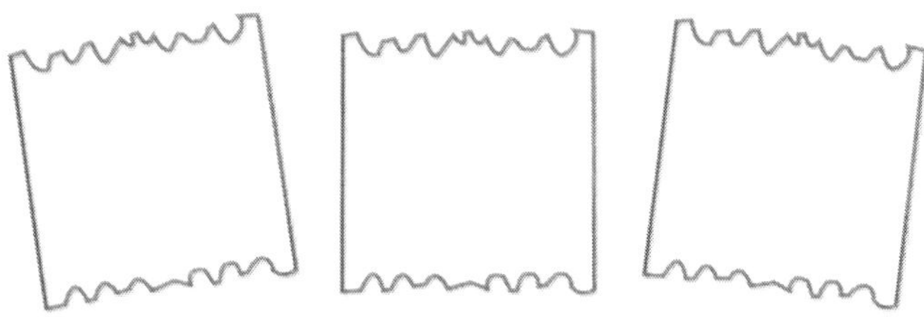

What Mattered in Sixth Grade

Our room lost the school softball championship when this cross-eyed kid popped out with the bases loaded. We did win the spelling bee, though. Weird Charlie said it was because we had the most girls.

The Scarlet Tanager edged out the Wood Duck in our balloting for the State Bird because the girls got organized when they found out the teacher liked red. I voted for the Bluejay. Weird Charlie voted for the Crow.

The teacher nearly got knocked out cold when a big portrait of somebody famous fell off the wall and conked her on the head. Most of the girls cried. Most of the boys laughed.

When we had to stand up and tell the class what we'd gotten for Christmas, Lisa Cohen started crying because she didn't get anything. It turned out she was Jewish.

The girls beat the boys in the school paper sale because one girl's father drove up with a huge truckload of bundles. It didn't seem to matter to the principal, who had told us more than once we had to do all the collecting and bundling by ourselves.

I was chosen to play Santa Claus for the third graders' class play which also got broadcast on television. At the station I got one of the newscasters to sign my autograph book, but when I brought it to school the next day, nobody knew who he was.

Anyone we didn't like was called a morphadike or just a morph, though we had no idea what that meant, not even Weird Charlie. One of the girls said that she and her friends knew but weren't ever going to tell us.

Our report cards changed for the third year in a row, this time with S's and V's and U's. I did best in reading, worst in penmanship and deportment, which was a word I hated. My mother said the teacher told her again in parent-teacher conferences that I was a hopeless daydreamer and they both were beginning to wonder if I'd ever grow out of it.

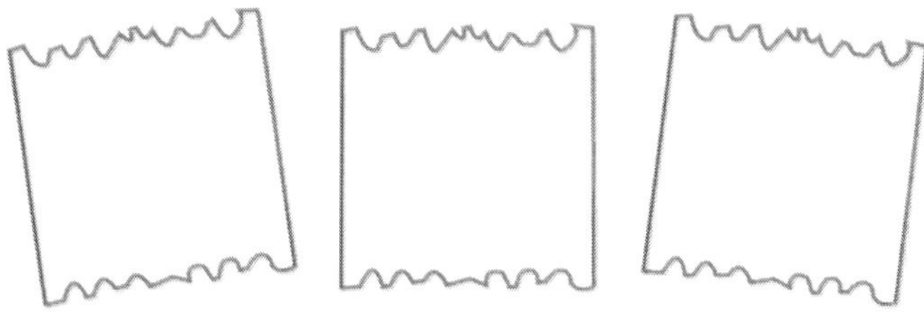

Someday, Maybe

My sister's new bicycle was shiny blue with long plastic streamers flowing from the handle grips. She'd gotten our father to take her somewhere to pick them out as soon as she could ride without training wheels. It was something special they had between them, from the time he taught her to ride, running beside her up and down the alley. It was something I'd probably never have because I didn't want to learn to ride a bike.

Maybe it was the fear of falling off or being laughed at, both of which happened the time my friend Paul tried to give me a ride on his big old Schwinn and could barely keep us moving. Most of the boys were getting some kind of English racer with those skinny little wheels I doubted I could ever handle. Or maybe it was just my stubbornness—things had just gone too far me to turn back, even if I was the only boy in the neighborhood who didn't have a bike. Thankfully, my best friend Pete would usually walk with me, even if it meant wheeling his bike along side of us. Someday, maybe, I'd learn to ride—if I could just find a bike that suited me and a place to practice with nobody else around.

At least my father never said anything about bikes, and I have to give my little sister credit, too, for never teasing me. But then, she didn't have to, not with those shiny streamers flowing from her handlebars as she pedaled past me down the street.

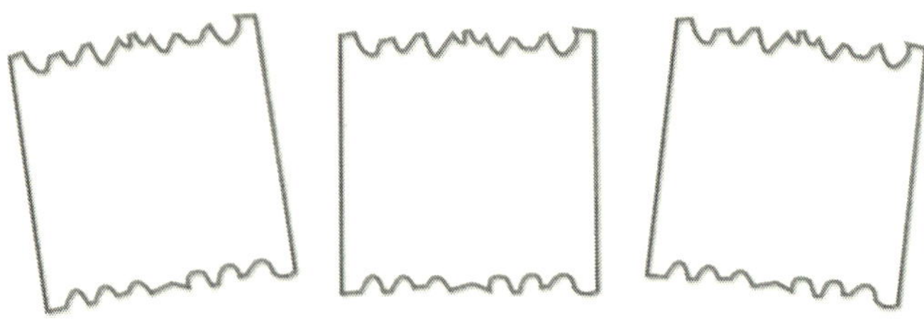

Good Sport

My father had been a really good athlete when he was growing up, and as hard as I tried I must have been a big disappointment—too fat, too slow, or maybe just too lazy. Even if he was out of town a lot, my father did get me a baseball bat and glove and showed me how to throw and catch, and bat—left-handed, like he did—and when I played one summer on the YMCA team he'd always ask me about the games even if he couldn't get to them. I never told him about being stuck out in right field where nobody ever hit it, not even me, because I'd usually swing late. I did say I got on base a lot, which was true, because most pitchers couldn't handle left-handed batters and I usually got walked or beaned. The one real base hit I remember was when I barely hit the ball off the end of the bat and it shot down the third base line, right up the third baseman's leg and into the air. He was as surprised as I was.

Basketball was pretty much the same thing—I always played center to clog up the lane, as the coach would say, and ended up getting knocked down and shooting a lot of free throws.

One thing my father did try to do was teach me how to swim, at one of the lakes in the city, where he decided we could start out from a deserted shore instead of the crowded bathing beach. But he didn't know about the drop-off, which wasn't very far out, and when he had to drag me from the water coughing and gasping, it pretty much ended my swimming lessons.

He was more successful at taking me to basketball games and listening to baseball on the radio with me. His enthusiasm taught me to love sports, and how to be a good sport, which he said was more important than anything. And I suppose that's what I was, getting up and dusting myself off, and somehow being willing to try one more time, even if I knew that soon enough I'd be picking myself up all over again.

Still Life with Ball and Glove

It was called Chicago Field because one side of its square block ran along Chicago Avenue, but its name always made me feel I was somewhere more important than a place only big enough for two baseball diamonds. Nicely located halfway between my best friend Pete's house and my own it became the place where we'd spend hours hitting baseballs to each other and sometimes even joining a pickup game. Whenever we said we were going to the park we knew that nobody was going to worry where we were or what we were doing.

It was the one place where nothing ever seemed to change, where we could imagine that many years in the future there'd still be a small group of boys yelling to chuck it here or get back for a deep one, which would be followed by the crack of a batted ball so dark from use it was be hard to pick up against the green of the trees. And even as it started getting late, there always seemed to be a little good light left before it was time to grab your gear and head for home, toward baths and beds and ballgames on the radio, and making plans for coming back tomorrow.

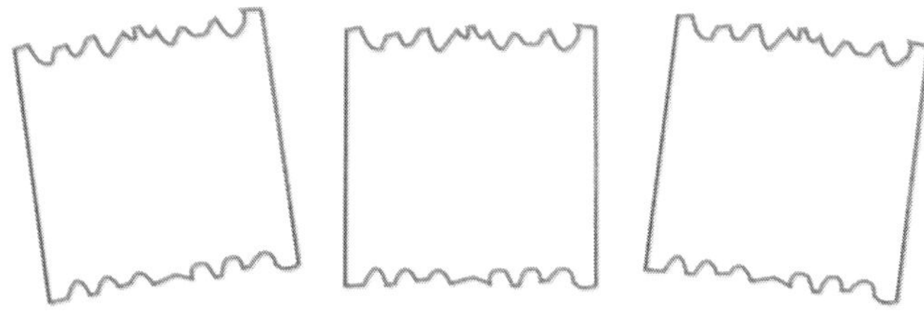

The Dream Squadron

My friend Pete and I spent a lot of time in the little hobby shop on 38th Street, looking through the shelves of plastic model airplane kits—Mustangs and B-29s and some of the newest jet fighters like the F-104. For awhile, every bit of money I could earn went into my model plane fund. Soon enough, my mother said my room looked like some kind of air museum, and how was she ever going to dust the planes I'd hung from the ceiling with thread? Someday, I told her, I was going to make bigger models, with engines, and then I was going to learn how to be a pilot of a real plane.

Each night as I was falling asleep, I'd watch those planes in the dim light of my room, hoping I'd have dreams about flying, though I never did. One summer day a couple of years later, when my friend Pete and I got especially bored, it seemed like a good idea to take down those dusty models and the other ones from the shelves and tape firecrackers to them and throw them out my bedroom window, cheering like crazy as they blew up in midair.

When he found out what happened, my father really surprised me by not getting mad about the firecrackers, though he did let me know he'd better not find any pieces of plastic in the grass. I still had one last model kit, a Sky Warrior, unassembled in the box, which I kept on my closet shelf for a long time—along with baseball cards and a jar of marbles, cowboy records, comic books and even a few packages of rock-hard bubblegum.

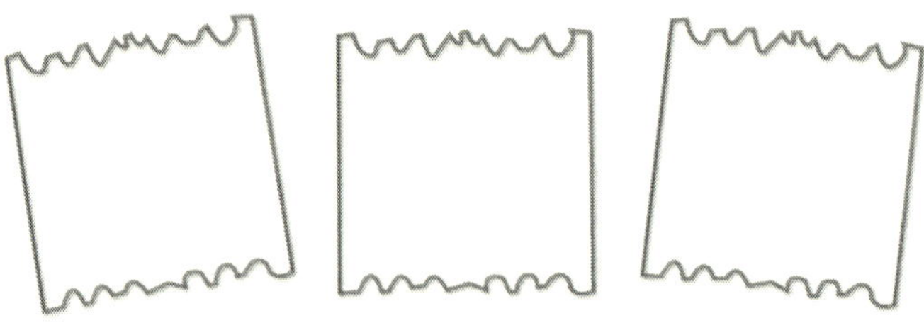

Endings

Besides firecrackers, the most important event of the summer in my grand-parents' small town was the county fair, which was held for three days around the Fourth of July. The fairgrounds were only a few blocks away, on the other side of the tracks, and it was easy enough to sneak into, under a barbed wire fence by one of the parking lots. The only hard thing to do was spread your money out over three days and not spend it all at once. My grandmother said that going without money would teach me a good lesson. My grandfather always found a way to slip me a few dimes and quarters whenever I ran out.

The only instructions I had were to keep away from the Midway games and eat at my grandparents' Lutheran church's tent. It didn't take long to figure out how crooked some of those games were. There was no way you could knock over all the bottles or get those rings on the posts, and the prizes you could win were nothing but junk—from the yo-yo that fell apart on the second spin to the ugly plaster statues nobody knew what to do with. Mostly, we'd just watch the grownups make fools of themselves and save our money for food and rides, and of course the side show, looking so exciting from the banners outside and so turning out to be so disappointing on the inside. Most of the stuff pictured on the banners wasn't even there, and what was, probably shouldn't have been, from the wrinkled knife thrower who didn't even come close to sticking one near his overweight assistant, to the Wild

Boy from Borneo in runny makeup, sitting in a pit of lifeless looking snakes and chewing on what was probably a chicken neck. The best thing was going on the rides--the rickety Ferris wheel with its huge greasy gears and wobbly seats, the terrifying Octopus it took at least two days to build the courage for, and our favorite, the Tilt-O-Whirl, which we rode over and over and then staggered like happy drunks in our dizziness.

One summer my cousin came to visit his grandmother, who was my great aunt, and came close to ruining things for me by winning a nice set of glasses at a church-sponsored bingo game while my friends and I were puking up forbidden pronto pups after finally taking on the Octopus. Even my grandfather looked disappointed when he heard the news, but the very next night he slipped me money for a submarine movie. It was that summer the movie theater started showing cinemascope and raised its prices, which also meant a lot of movies not even my grandfather would allow me to go to.

It was, as it turned out, the last summer I'd get to go to the county fair or anywhere else in my grandparents' town, the last summer they'd be in the white house with the porch swing and the huge gardens, the last summer of my grandfather's life. After that, when I'd think of him, for some reason I'd always remember the county fair and the last Ferris Wheel rides of the evening, when there weren't many people left at the fairgrounds and most of the seats were empty, lurching and rocking as one by one the last passengers got off and nobody got on to replace them.

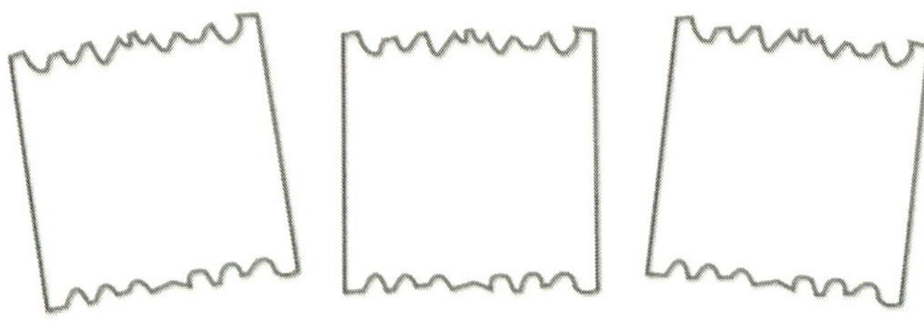

And Never Forget It

I don't remember how the news came. It was probably a long distance call late at night, which almost always meant that something bad had happened. However it came, when my grandfather died in the spring of my first year of junior high it was about the worst news I could imagine.

Why they decided to have the funeral at a place not far from where we lived and not in the small town where he and my grandmother lived I could never figure out, except maybe it was easier for everybody to come to it. And most of them came to our house after the service—my uncle and two aunts, cousins I'd never met as well as some I had, friends and neighbors and former patients, for my grandfather had been a small town doctor and just about everybody loved him. I can't remember much of the funeral service except that I tried hard not to cry, until I saw my uncle and some of the other grown men crying, and then afterwards, my Aunt Molly having too many cocktails, as she usually did, asking my mother over and over just who was going to keep Grandma in line now. Whenever she saw me she'd ask me the same question, too, about whether I thought I could grow up to be half as good a man as her dad was, and when I'd answer no, I didn't think I could, she'd say, "You bet your boots, buster, and never forget it!" Then she'd start in all over again.

It was a couple of hours before people started leaving our house and I spent most of it trying to keep away from my aunt, though I did hear a lot of stories, too. But while just about everyone was telling stories about my grandfather, I can't remember anybody asking me to tell one, or even asking how much I was going to miss him—which was all right, I suppose, because I knew that was a question I was a long way from being able to answer.

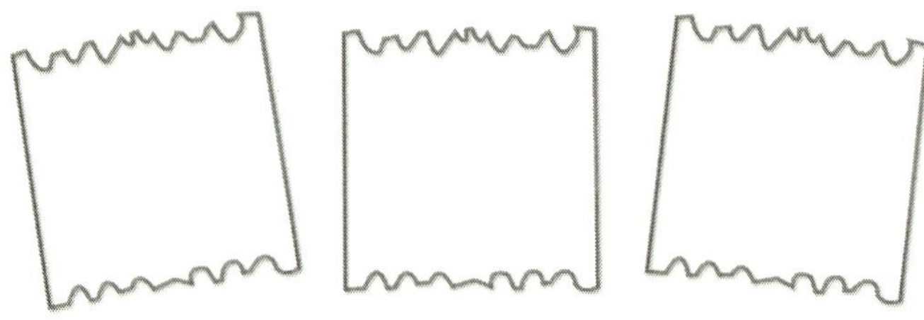

Bread-Winner

A young couple with a toddler rented the top floor of the house next door and even if I was barely into my teens they decided I'd make a good baby sitter, which I didn't really want to do, though it did give me a chance to earn some money, which especially pleased my father.

The man, whose name was Don, had just about everything I wanted to have someday—a big TV and an impressive gun collection and sporty blue Buick, which he usually parked on the street right behind my father's plain black Ford. Don washed his car every week and waxed it once a month, sometimes letting me help him polish all that chrome. He also played for a local softball team, so we talked about baseball too, and whether we'd ever get a major league team. Especially after being around Don, I kept asking my father when we could get a new car, but since he got a car for trips at work, he really didn't need more than that old Ford. I knew if I kept after him he'd eventually ask me why I just didn't move in with Don. That was my father's way.

After school started in the fall things got pretty busy and I didn't think about not being called to babysit at Don's. When I finally realized I hadn't seen his car lately, my mother told me Don's wife and little girl had gone to stay with relatives and that Don had been having some trouble at his job and they had to let the apartment go. She didn't know where he had ended up, only that the movers had come one day when I was in school the week before.

I knew my father wasn't really very happy in his own job, especially not with all the traveling he had to do, but being a good bread-winner, as he liked to call it, was just about the most important thing he could do. The first time I heard that expression I had to laugh—it made me think of wining a loaf of bread on a TV quiz show or something. But the more I thought about it, the more I wondered if I'd ever be able to do what my father had done for his family. I supposed that somehow I'd learn, though I also hoped I would have a better car than that old black Ford.

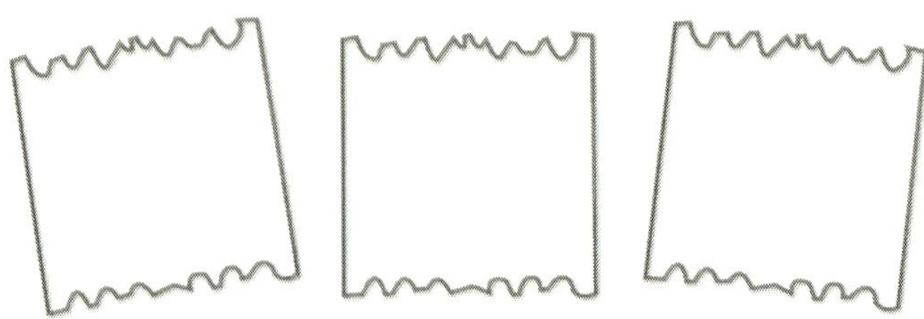

Contenders

Just about the most fun I had the summer after my grandfather died and we didn't make the trip to his town anymore was to go to baseball games with my friend Pete at the old ballpark about a mile from where I lived. It didn't matter that the home team was in the minor leagues, not when we could stand out on Nicollet Avenue on the other side of that short right field fence and try to snag balls during batting practice. We knew all the players' names and a lot of the statistics too, and even if we understood the best players could be called up to the big leagues at any time, there always seemed to be a new guy who'd step right in and do a great job. Sometimes I really wished my father would be able to take me to a game, but even if he couldn't, he still liked to listen on the radio and we could always talk a little about our team, the Millers.

The best thing about that team was the way they were always contenders, all the way to winning the Little World Series, as the championship was called, their last game in the old ballpark. The next year they played in a new stadium way out in the suburbs, built to attract some major league team, my father said. After that, both of us lost some of our interest, though sometimes we'd still listen to a game together at the kitchen table—him reading the newspaper and sipping a beer and me with *Sport* magazine or maybe my stamp album. Sometimes I'd ask him which of the major league teams might want to move to our city, but he said he couldn't guess. Even if one did, it would take a long time to be as special as the one that used to play at Nicollet Field.

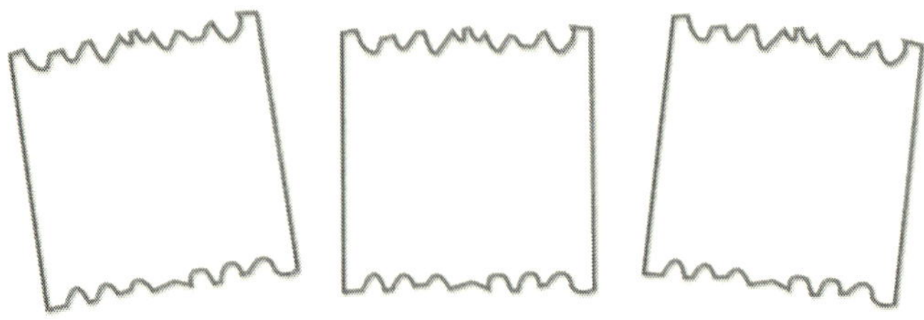

The Hero as Lumberjack

At the start of our family vacation during the summer after sixth grade, we stayed with some of my mother's cousins in Wisconsin and then we all went to visit another set of relatives on a farm, which was going to be pretty boring until my cousin Jane, who was a year older and starting to get good looking, decided to ride with us in our car. I was starting to think a lot about girls and really liked the idea of going anywhere with Jane, even if she was my cousin.

There were so many people having coffee in the farmhouse that Jane and I were given bottles of Coke and sent out to visit this old man who was some sort of cousin and didn't care much about the visiting relatives. He was working out in this big woodshed, where he told me I could chop some logs with his axe while Jane should come and sit on his lap. It made me feel especially good to swing that axe like a lumberjack while Jane was watching and that old cousin sat there winking and grinning too. It wasn't till we were in the backseat together on the ride home that Jane whispered what she was thinking about me. "Didn't you see?" she asked. "That filthy old man made me put my hand down on his *thing* and how was I supposed to I get out with you in the doorway swinging that stupid axe?"

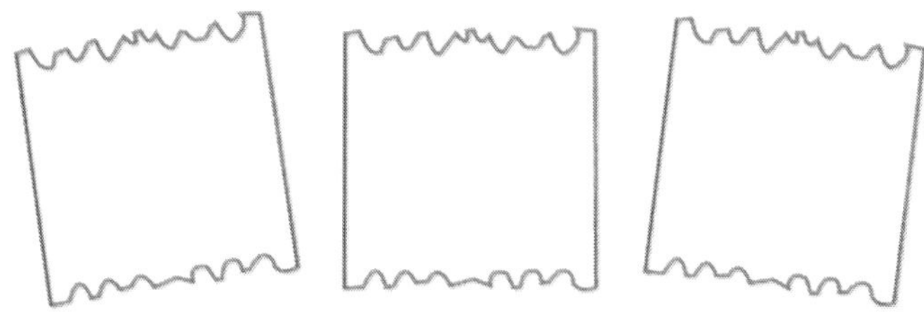

Practice Makes Perfect

I don't know why that trumpet looked so good to me in sixth grade. It wasn't the idea of playing music—my mother had tried for years to get me to take piano lessons. Maybe I thought girls liked trumpets or maybe it was the way a trumpet player could strike a pose—a lot cooler than a trombone player, for example, even though my father had played trombone in high school and said it was an instrument I would probably like. Whatever the reason, I had to have that shiny trumpet—had to have my parents rent it, that is, so I could be signed up for beginner's band. Maybe I thought I could just pick it up and begin to play it right away. It really looked like that might be possible. I hadn't counted on all that practice, on trying build up my lip by buzzing into the mouthpiece day after day and then still making those horrible blats and honks.

Seventh grade was worse because I didn't seem to be getting very much better and because of the band teacher, who yelled at us a lot and who also thought we needed to listen to his idea of good music. So besides signing our practice sheets our parents had to sign a paper saying we'd watched the opera singers on the *Voice of Firestone* or what was almost worse, *The Lawrence Welk Show*, which I had to keep a secret from my friends who weren't in band. I was also beginning to think that maybe I'd simply picked the wrong instrument. Guitars were just as cool as trumpets, weren't they?

Maybe a big tenor sax, a snare drum, or even a xylophone. There had to be something out there I could be really good at—if I could only find out what it was.

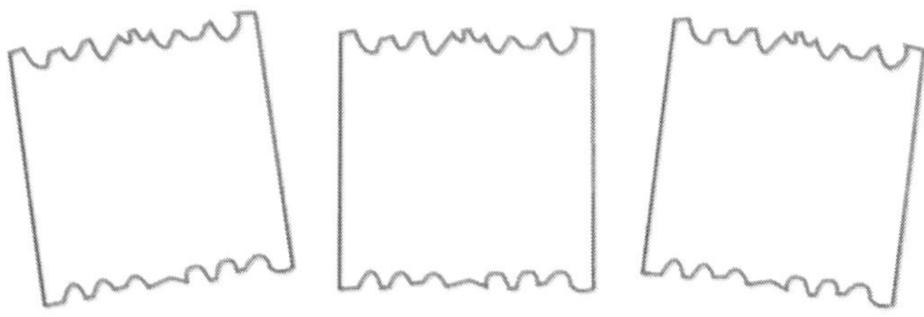

The Main Event

A lot of us watched wrestling on TV but the really good matches never got televised—they were only talked about, to get bigger crowds to the auditorium on weekends. Most of us knew that wrestling was supposed to be completely fake but we got really interested any way, especially when the Russian Kamalkov brothers came to town and started beating up all the American tag-teams. Eventually, of course, an American team won, and then it was Japanese wrestlers who took over as the bad guys. That was when my friend Pete's mother got free wrestling tickets from the place she worked and gave them to the two of us.

It was supposed to be a world championship match between a Japanese guy named Shabuya, or something like that, and an American who was so uninteresting I had trouble remembering his name. In any case, we had tremendous seats in the fifth or sixth row, where we could hear and see everything going on in the ring. The only thing that seemed real to us was the sweat on the wrestlers' bodies. My little sister could have figured out that the holds and the punches were pretty much a total fake, that there was a lot more noisy slamming of the canvas than anything else.

By the time we got to the main event of the evening—the Japanese vs. American in the the so-called world championship—Pete and I had gotten so disgusted we decided to start cheering for the Japanese guy, which was something that surprised even that wrestler, looking from time to time into the audience to see who was stupid enough to scream for the wrong man.

Shabuya lost, of course, and the only thing our cheering brought us was the anger of the fans in the seats nearby. Pete got some Coke poured on his head and I got swatted with something, probably an umbrella. It didn't take us long to decide we'd better shut up if we wanted to get out of that place alive.

As we waited for our bus a couple of people recognized us and called us Jap-lovers or traitors as they walked by, and even if we didn't say much to each other on the way home, we both knew we wouldn't be talking about the wrestling match in Home Room on Monday, or any match, for a long, long time.

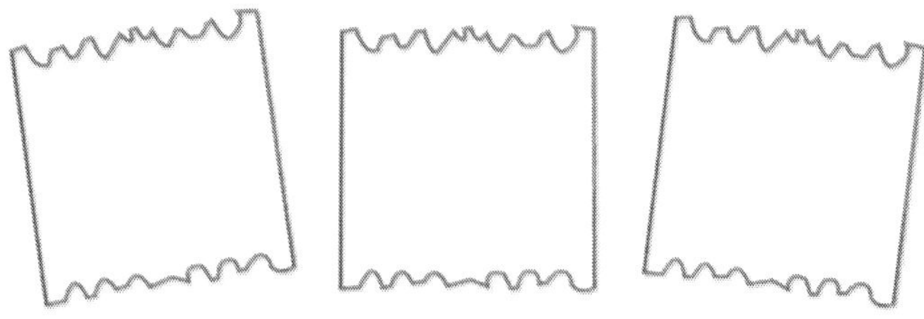

Going to the Bottom

My grandmother held my hand so tightly I couldn't feel anything in my fingers, telling me for blocks and blocks she was going to rewrite her will, ever since I got her on the midnight bus in front of my aunt's apartment building. She kept her mouth right next to my ear and it reeked of whiskey and heavy perfume. I felt more and more like I needed to throw up, but she wouldn't let go of my hand, even when I told her our stop was coming up and I had to look out the window for the right street. She kept saying I was such a good boy, collaring me for her droolly kisses, and that taking care of her was just what Jesus would want me to do.

I didn't really know what Jesus had to do with it. I only hoped nobody I knew would ever see me like this. And then, instead of letting go, she told me one more time that I was her delight for helping her home on the bus after all the terrible things my aunt and my mother had done to her, and never to have children of my own because they would stab me in the back.

I was even more afraid of what my mother and my Aunt might be doing to each other right then, or what they'd do to me, later, when they found out I was the one who took Grandma home on the bus after all their screaming had frightened me, after the screaming and glass-breaking and names they kept calling each other. I kept telling my sister to come with us, but she was just too little to understand what was going on, especially when my aunt kept giving her ice cream and Coke. She didn't want to understand the screaming and the rest of it, only that it was some kind of game where she kept winning all the prizes. As long as they let her stay up and watch TV and eat sweets, everything was okay with her.

When Grandma went after the Kleenexes in her purse, I was finally able to get my hand free and rub some life back into my fingers, and then it was time for our stop, time to pull the cord and get her on her feet and down the back steps of the bus, out into the chilly April air and those two long blocks till we were safely inside the house. She kept asking me if I knew it was Easter and I told her yes, I knew all about Easter, when Jesus died for our sins, and I wished hard I *could* pray to Jesus, but I couldn't, not even on Easter, which, they all kept reminding me was the holiest day of the year. I couldn't, not even after church and Sunday school and a huge ham dinner at my aunt's apartment, with Easter baskets and presents and not getting yelled at for watching as much TV or eating as many sweets as we wanted.

And then there was what I imagined as I sat in the dark of my room— about Jesus the Fisher of Men gliding across the water while the rest of us were in a sinking boat. Everybody was calling to Jesus, who just stood there smiling and watching, while we all were calling out and yelling at each other at the same time, and there was glass breaking and locked doors and long rides home on the bus and all of us going to the bottom, even on Easter, the holiest day of the year, right to the very bottom.

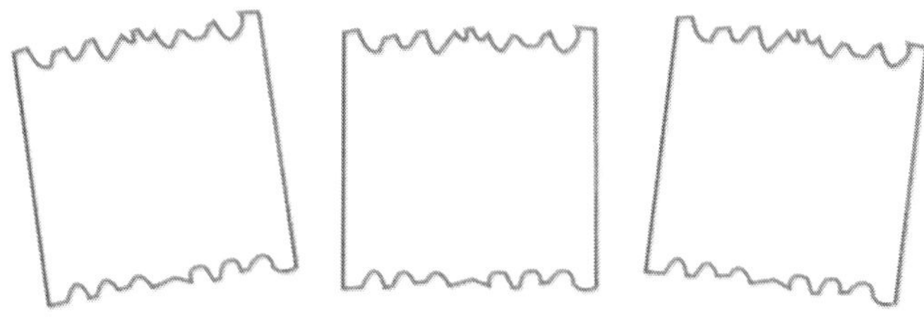

Unhappy Camper

One Sunday not long after Easter the preacher of our church got pretty excited telling everyone about the summer camp our church was going in with some others to open at a lake only a couple of hours away. He went on and on about how it was all parents' Christian duty to send their children for a week or two at camp, where the kids would not only get to swim and hike and all the other things you usually did at camp, they'd get daily religious instruction as well.

Maybe it was because my grandfather had just died and I couldn't go to his town for the summer anymore, or maybe my parents just needed a break, I was one of the first kids that got signed up for camp. A couple of weeks after school was out in June, my parents drove me to this place in the deep woods full of unpleasant looking buildings by a small lake. I stayed with five other boys in a cabin with so many holes in the screens there were usually more bugs inside than out.

One of those boys was named Eddie, who'd been in my math class at school. He was the first friend I made, and just about the only one, because he had firecrackers in his suitcase and two packs of Winston cigarettes he'd swiped from his mom. It didn't take long to find out we were the only ones in the cabin who had any interest in learning how to smoke, which we did out in the woods at every opportunity. Besides smoking, we played a lot of ping pong, stood around in the water when we were supposed to be learning how to swim, and even got the rest of the cabin telling dirty jokes after lights out. I had to admit, camp was turning out better than I'd expected, but about then I started to itch like crazy from a bad case of poison ivy, which I'd probably gotten out in the woods with Eddie. It didn't get really bad till my parents brought me home, where I ended up in bed for a couple of days. I couldn't help feeling it was all some kind of punishment for being so sinful at camp. I even had some nightmares about being dragged off to hell's fires—which smelled suspiciously like the smoke from Eddie's Winston cigarettes.

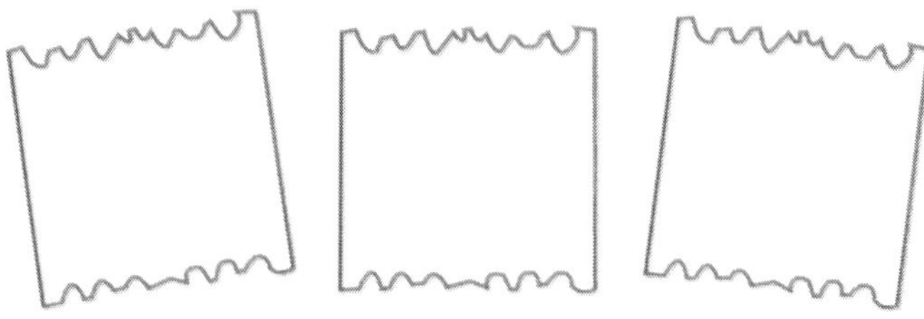

Market Share

In seventh grade, our math teacher decided we should learn something about the stock market. Each of us would get a thousand imaginary dollars to spend on our choice of imaginary stocks, then watch the prices for a month, with a prize for the person with biggest gain. I'd never heard the term Blue Chips, but that's what I chose, my father told me later—Standard Oil, General Motors, Westinghouse, names that sounded so substantial. I raced home each afternoon to wait for the newspaper to see how my stocks had done, and by the end of the month I'd made almost a hundred dollars, the best of anyone I talked to.

But the day we figured our final gains and losses in class, it turns out that this guy with thick glasses and who never talked to anyone had tripled his money on wildcat oil well drilling and silver mines. In fact, I wasn't even in the top five, all my fantasies of someday being a big success in the business world melting away. The teacher said our next math lesson would be about making a budget and balancing a checkbook—with more of that money I somehow knew I going to have a hard time getting.

At Arm's Length

Margaret's mousy hair hung down in stringy clumps, her skin had a kind of gray tint to it, and she chewed her pencils till they splintered into little pieces. Then she'd chew her nails, though there really wasn't much left to chew. Every so often she'd turn around and ask what I was doing, or maybe she'd just stare, roll her eyes, and smile, like we shared some kind of secret, maybe because we shared the same initials in our names—all three of them! That's why, when our seventh grade science teacher decided to seat our class alphabetically, Margaret ended up in the desk in front of me.

I kept telling her to turn around and keep her stupid face out of my business, but no matter what I said to her, she' d eventually be staring in my direction again. Once, when I was daydreaming, I even shouted at her, and then the teacher raised her voice to tell me to behave myself and quit bothering Margaret. For days I had to avoid the grins of kids in that class, especially those pretty girls who could lose me in daydreams with a single glance—the ones who brushed past me in the hallways like I wasn't even there. I had to wonder if those girls ever teased each other about boys the way we boys could tease each other about girls. I knew for sure that Margaret's weirdness would make a great story to tell my friends, but I also knew what would happen if I ever mentioned anything about her.

I never saw of Margaret outside of that one class, and all I really knew about her was that she didn't hang out in any groups. She didn't even seem to have any interest in the other girls, just in bothering me, rolling her stupid eyes and grinning her lopsided grin, always reminding me about the things I didn't want to think about.

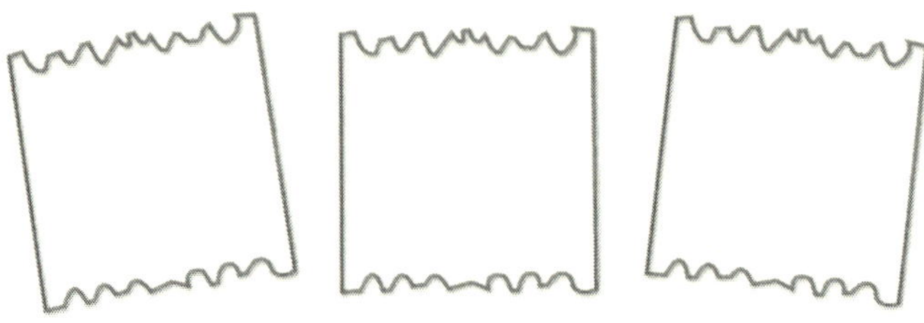

Forbidden Fruit

There were two apple trees in our backyard, one of which was a flowering crab, whose small, sour apples were a lot better for throwing than for eating. The other tree grew regular-sized green apples, but there weren't many of them and they seemed limited to the highest branches. After a lot of experimenting, my father and I figured out a way to knock most of them into a coffee can nailed to a long pole.

Several other yards for blocks in every direction had trees with far better apples, deliciously green and sour, which led to the most daring events of the summer—the apple raids.

A group of us would meet out behind Paul's garage next door each afternoon to plan our strategy for the evening—where we'd go, the dangers we might run into, the escape route and eventual meeting place to divide and eat our loot. We had only two rules—never to hit the same tree twice and keep quiet if you ever got caught, though there really wasn't much possibility of that. Once or twice people did come out and yell at us, but mostly we'd simply sneak into a yard, grab a few apples off the tree and then take off, laughing so hard we could barely run. Dogs were the scariest possibilities, but only once were we ever chased by a dog, and then saved by his extra-long chain which we'd never even noticed. As it turned out, the most exciting part of the apple raids was telling the story afterwards, gorging ourselves on apples and then, as it was getting dark, heading home riding on each other's laughter and good wishes, heaving apple cores at streetlights and garbage cans and sometimes at each other, already making our plans the next raid, and the next.

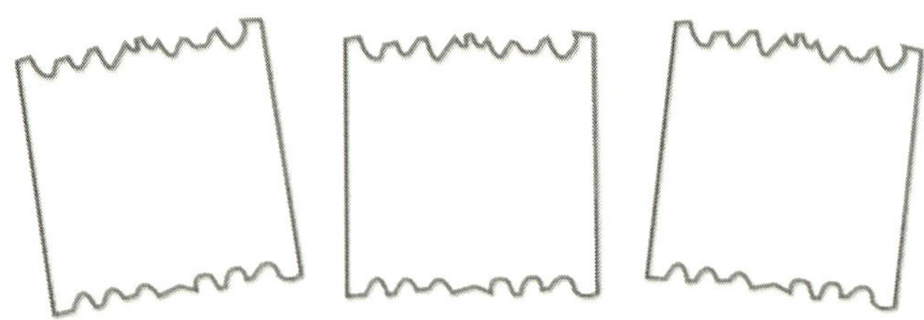

Field Hand

I don't know how it happened but somebody decided I should spend some time on my great uncle Minnie's farm. It was probably my grandmother, who had said for a long time how country life was a lot better than city life, but in any case I found myself being dropped off at her brother's farm way over on the North Dakota border. Fortunately, my cousin Jack was just about my age so I did have someone to talk to—and we did get along better than I'd expected, especially when he decided he'd teach me how to drive.

They were combining wheat when I arrived and like one of his older brothers, Jack drove one of the big grain trucks up beside the combine's spout to be filled up with wheat and then taken to be unloaded at the big elevator in town. My job was to climb up in the bed of the truck with a scoop shovel and keep the load even, which wasn't very hard work but was dusty and gross since a lot of chopped-up grasshoppers came out with the wheat and sometimes other chopped-up stuff, like snakes and mice. Thanks to all the heavy machinery, farming was a lot more dangerous than I'd imagined. Jack had a lot of stories about farmers who'd gotten caught in machines and several of the men he knew were missing fingers, including one of my other cousins.

Our driving lessons would take place when we'd get some break time. Jack would sit behind the wheel of the empty grain truck, set the throttle and then we'd switch places so I could turn the wheel and drive us in loopy, bumpy circles through the stubble field. I couldn't wait to tell my friends back home, hoping I could be cool and let it slip our casually but knowing I'd most likely blurt it out the first time I saw them.

Once combining was over there wasn't nearly as much to do, but my great aunt found plenty to keep us busy, like shucking corn or weeding her gigantic garden. Probably the best thing about farming was the food—not just that there was so much of it but that it tasted so good after working outdoors. Sometimes at the dinner table—dinner was the noon meal not the evening one like at home—someone would joke that they'd make a farmer out of me yet. I always said sure, they might be able to do that, but the longer I stayed on the farm the more I was finding out it was already too late for me. I couldn't even find my way to town or the place where so-and-so's farm was in relation to my uncle's, even though I'd been over those roads dozens of times. I didn't know about crops or machinery or animals either, and I couldn't help but think my cousin would have a lot easier time in the city than I did on the farm. But Jack never got tired of saying how much he disliked big cities, at least the ones he'd been to, like Grand Forks. By the time I left my uncle's place, I was sure of two things—that they'd never make a farmer out of me and that I was going to do whatever I could to keep all my parts attached to me.

A Trip to Wonderland

Sometime between seventh and eighth grade I needed a physical for school and my father took me to this old doctor who used to live in his hometown, probably to save some money. After the exam, when I was getting dressed, I heard my father outside the door telling the doctor he was getting more and more concerned about my weight problem. That doctor really surprised me when he said he had an idea it might be related to my Thyroid gland and to bring me back for some kind of test a few days later.

It turned out that doctor as right, and when he put me on some pills I started losing weight like crazy, even though I was eating pretty much like I always did. It was as if my fantasy about a blubber-stripping machine had finally come true.

The problem was that I started growing too—a whole inch in the first month—and by the time I didn't need the pills anymore, some of the kids were calling me Bean Pole and Stretch. Even worse, I'd lost a lot of coordination too. It seemed like I could fall down just trying to tie my shoes.

I couldn't help thinking about Alice in Wonderland, growing till her head hit the ceiling, then shrinking till she was the size of a mouse. It was like somebody couldn't figure out what size I was supposed to be, either. Maybe they'd start me on a different kind of pills one day. Till then, I'd have to get used to that strange person staring back in the mirror, the gangly one with a nose that looked a couple of sizes too big for his face.

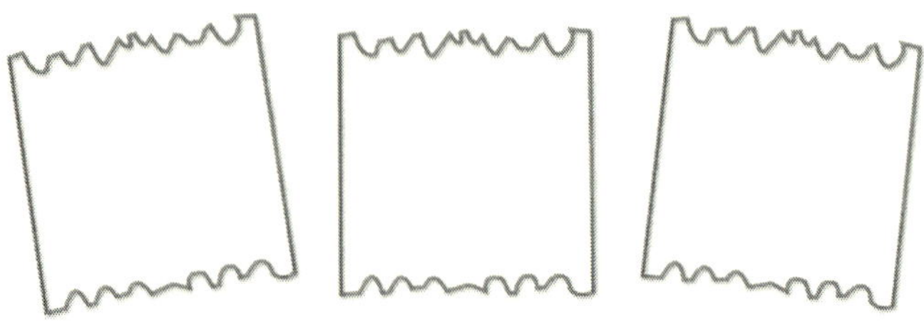

In Training

My father had played a lot of basketball in school and a couple of times he took me to games—at the university when we lived near it, and later downtown to see the big professional stars like George Mikan and Slater Martin. Once I started losing weight and growing taller, basketball looked like the sport I might have some chance of being good at, and it didn't take my father long to put up a backboard and hoop on the garage of our new house, where I practiced shooting baskets for at least an hour every day.

My junior high didn't have a team but there was a pretty good church league, even though our little congregation had just merged with a much bigger one which had its own team already established. So, when they formed a second team it was mostly made up of new kids or the ones who'd been cut from the other team. Amazingly, we did manage to win half of our games that year, but our real purpose was to scrimmage with the church's A Team, the one that got all the attention and could beat us by 20 points without really trying.

That was the winter I'd started Confirmation classes, too, which pleased my parents but really bothered me. Every lesson started with "We should fear and love God," with our Norwegian pastor always coming down hard on the side of *fear*, threatening damnation for just about everything, but especially lust and self-abuse. Besides being required to play basketball even when I wanted to quit, I had to shovel church sidewalks and light the altar candles each Sunday for one of the services. It had started out simply enough, with basketball, but there was no telling where it was going to lead. The business of salvation was a lot more complicated than I'd ever imagined.

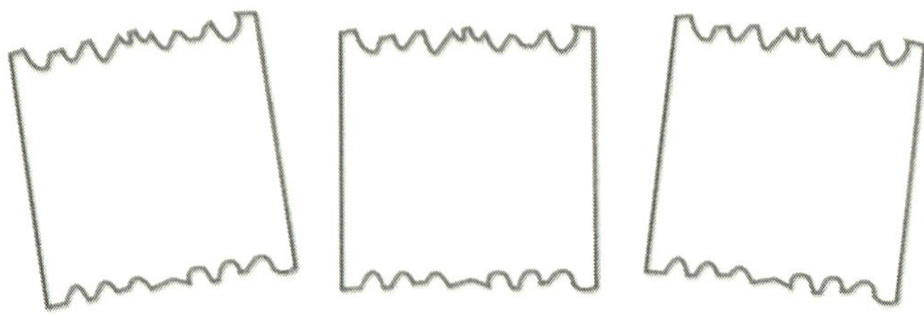

The Last Hunt

One Friday evening at dinner my father announced that he'd decided to take me hunting the next morning, so we'd have to go to bed early and be up before dawn. After my grandfather died, I inherited one of my grandfather's shotguns—the little .20 gauge single shot. My father had taken me out in the country to practice shooting a couple of times but the next morning was going to be a real pheasant hunt with three of the men from his office.

When my father and I got to the farm one of those men's relatives owned, the sun hadn't been up very long but everyone had been waiting for us to get there. Mainly we walked the edges of some corn fields, two of the men on each side and me by myself, quite a way behind my father and his friend. We'd been doing this most of the morning without seeing a single bird when suddenly a cock pheasant lifted directly across my path not 20 yards in front of me. A little amazed at my own coolness, I followed the bird along the barrel of the gun and squeezed—not jerked—the trigger, just the way my father had shown me. But nothing happened. The bird was gone and the useless gun was heavy in my hands.

When I caught up with my father and the others, they discovered that the shell in the gun clearly had a dent in the percussion cap but it hadn't gone off. One of the men took the shell out and left it on a fencepost and one of the others kept asking me how big the bird was and then chuckling. My father didn't say much of anything other than we should get rid of all that old ammo that had come with the gun, and then he just shook his head. As we walked into the chilly afternoon after stopping for sandwiches and cups of hot soup from thermoses, I couldn't help thinking about those pictures of my father and grandfather on hunting trips in North Dakota before I was born, with dozens of pheasants lined up on the ground in front of them as they knelt with their shotguns and smiled into the camera. It was getting pretty clear that I'd never have a picture like that with my father, especially since that farm got sold later in the fall and I heard my father saying it was just about the last good place he knew of where they could get permission to hunt.

I knew that some of the men still probably didn't believe me about that pheasant I shot at, but I could still see it so clearly, and sometimes that dud shell, too—sitting there on the fencepost, waiting to go off.

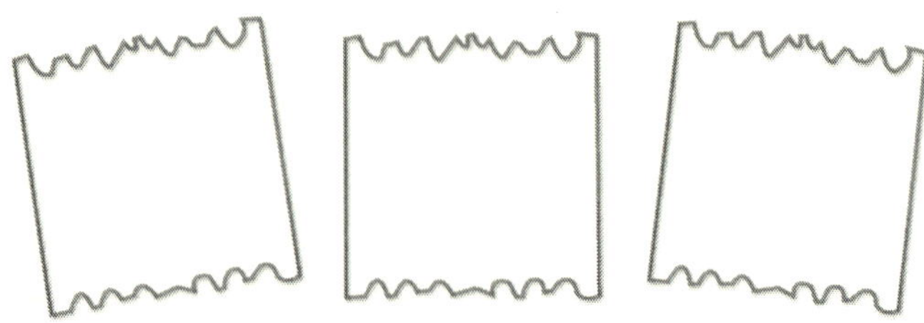

Generations

Even before I started school, my mother and I listened to *Don MacNeill's Breakfast Club* on the radio every morning. I really liked the music he played, especially when it was March Time and I could stomp around the living room swinging my arms like a soldier. I loved my Saturday morning programs too, especially the one sponsored by Buster Brown Shoes with Froggy the Gremlin, and when I got a little older there was *Oxydol's Own Ma Perkins*, which I'd listen to with my mother when I walked home from school for lunch. Some nights I'd get to hear *The Lone Ranger, Sergeant Preston of the Yukon,* and *The Shadow,* though my mother didn't like that last one because it could give me bad dreams.

My father always listened to the news with Cedric Adams on WCCO radio, and my grandfather liked the one that started with "Good evening, Mr. and Mrs. America and all the ships at sea." It amazed me that people way out on some ocean might be listening to the same radio station we were. When I got older, and after we got our first TV, I'd lie in bed most nights and listen to the ballgames on that same radio, which my grandmother gave me after my grandfather died. I could tell that for the out-of-town games our announcer wasn't really at the ballpark, just sitting in his studio reading what was happening and trying to make it sound dramatic. He played crowd noise in the background to make it seem real but the cheering usually came in all the wrong places.

The best thing about having my own radio was that nobody told me what to listen to, though I did get told not to blast the volume. My favorite station was WLOL, which played the best music, like the Coasters and Bill Haley and the Comets. Every time I heard the term Disc Jockey it made me imagine this guy riding a giant record like it was a horse. That's what I liked about the radio, the way it made you imagine things. I had to feel sorry for my little sister, who couldn't remember when we didn't have a TV set and missed all those good radio shows. Instead, she parked herself in front of the TV whenever she could—till somebody came and turned it off and made her go outside and play.

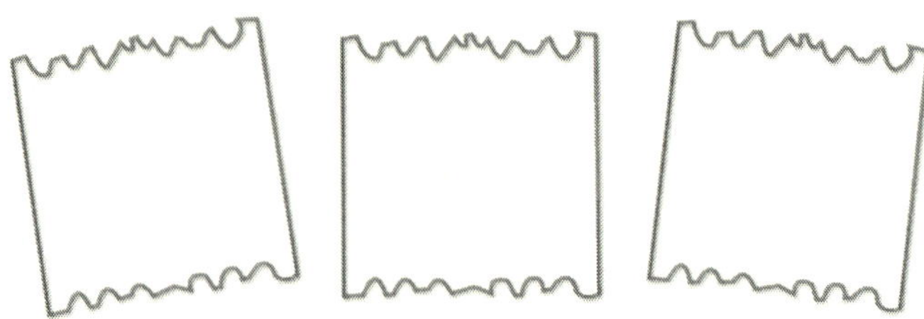

Bazooms

"What's the strongest thing in the world?" Bergy used to ask. "A bra," he'd say, falling down on the grass. "Because it holds up two milk factories." That was the funniest joke I'd ever heard, at eleven anyway. "Bazooms," Bergy would say, waving his fingers in circles and rolling his eyes. Bazooms, like in his *National Geographic*s.

I hadn't seen Bergy in quite awhile but I always thought of him when the subject of bazooms came up. It was hard to believe that the girls in our class would ever grow up like that, except for maybe Shari across the street who was a year older and some of the tenth graders were starting to come over and take her for rides on their bikes. Shari had real bazooms, like those ladies we'd watch in the grocery store every day, bending for stuff on the lower shelves. "Ain't summer great," my friend Pete said, and each night we'd walk my dog around every block in the neighborhood, looking for bazooms in windows. We never did see any, but my father said how nice it was to see me take some responsibility for a change, that maybe I was learning something after all and he sure hoped it wasn't going to change. "Not a chance," Pete said, and rolled his eyes at me, but all I was thinking about was Shari's dark window and those stupid bikes in her front yard.

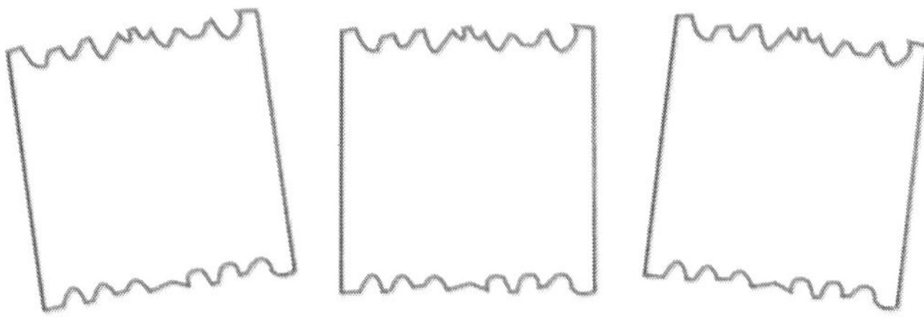

Industrial Arts

In the seventh and eighth grades, all the boys had to take shop classes, while the girls took Home Ec. Some of the boys mysteriously got auto mechanics but most of us had to start with mechanical drawing, which was taught by the meanest teacher I'd ever been around—a short, bald-headed man with forearms like Popeye's. Rumor had it he'd been a professional wrestler and then lost half his stomach from being wounded in Korea. Whatever his past was, he seemed to be angry all the time, and about once a week he'd pick somebody to beat up. I don't remember much about mechanical drawing itself, just about keeping my head down and looking busy while the teacher dragged some poor kid down the aisle, slapping him on the ears with his free hand and yelling that he was going to teach us all some manners. Whatever I did, I didn't get beat up, and most of us ended up in Metal Shop the next semester, though I did hear later that the big brother of one of those kids went after that mechanical drawing teacher with a tire iron in the parking lot one day after school.

The Metal Shop teacher was a soft-spoken white-haired man who some-times seemed to forget where he was. We all ended up making fishing floats for our fathers by soldering cans together. None of us had fathers who fished, and most of us never took home those floats, just ditched them in the big trash can by the parking lot. The best part of class was when we got to make aluminum ashtrays on the turning lathe. My mother was really impressed with mine, though soon enough it ended up in a drawer, along with half the other stuff I'd ever made in school and brought home.

In eighth grade, Woodworking and Electricity were the other shop courses we'd have to take, and I had to wonder what kind of junk I'd be making that would end up in that drawer. At least I hadn't heard about any of those teachers beating kids up in class.

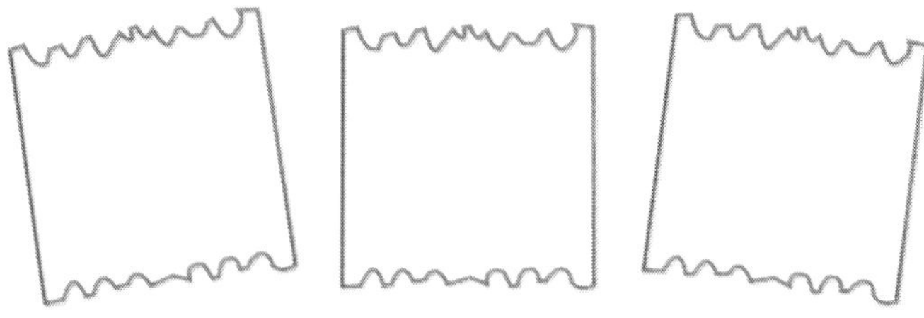

The Performing Arts

As long as I could remember, grownups seemed to think one of the best things kids could do was take part in some kind of show. Some of the worst were Christmas programs at church, especially the ones where I had to recite a Bible verse. When I got a little older I'd have to play a shepherd in the manger scene, wearing a stupid bathrobe with a dishtowel tied around my head. I kind of wanted to be one of the Three Kings, who had a lot neater costumes, but I never got chosen.

In grade school, our class would have to sing in programs sometimes, and when I played in the junior high band we'd give at least two concerts a year, and most of the time my parents would come. They could even see me up on stage because I played the baritone—there were only four of us, sitting toward the front. My band teacher had asked me to change instruments because he had way too many trumpet players. At least I didn't get picked for the sousaphone, which seemed nearly impossible to carry those two or three times we had to march in parades. I was glad, too, that I wasn't good enough to get chosen to play a concert solo.

Sometimes I'd have to take part in other programs at school, like the one for Armistice Day, when the boys in my English class had to stand behind the curtain and recite "Flanders Fields." I thought my English teacher was going to flunk us all because we couldn't keep from giggling. Mostly, though, all I had to do was play in the band. Lugging my baritone from school in its clunky case or out on the playground learning how to march in straight rows, I'd try to remember how proud my parents were at my band concerts. Or maybe they were just happy that I seemed to be keeping out of trouble, that I was doing anything at all.

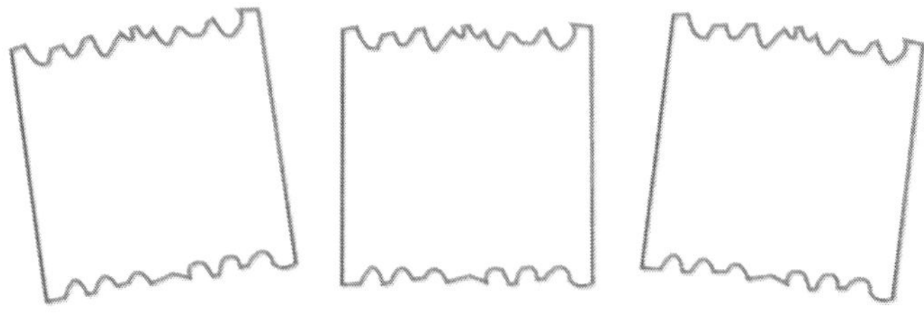

Physical Education

Rumor had it that the eighth grade Phys Ed teacher was a drunk. Jerry Manrud said he'd seen him in his little office next to the gym taking swigs of something in a paper bag but nobody really believed Jerry till the day Mr. Swenson was yelling at the swimming class from the diving board and lost his balance and fell in, and then he tried to demonstrate some swimming strokes—like he'd meant to be in the water all along. Most of the time we didn't have any swimming lessons. The three days a week we were in the pool it was usually "free swim" all hour, meaning the boys who could swim spent most of their time terrorizing those of us who couldn't in the shallow end. It was the same for basketball or any other sport. A lot of the time Mr. Swenson stayed in his office from just after he took attendance until it was time to blow his whistle and get us to the showers. A lot of the time we played a game called War, where the even-numbered squads lined up on one side of the gym, the odd-numbered ones on the other and then we all scrambled for the box of volleyballs in the middle, so we could "kill" the other team with a ball. You were lucky not to get hit in the head with one of the basketballs that somehow got put in the box, or worse, kicked silly by one of the hoods who, after awhile, didn't even bother changing into their gym shorts and tennis shoes. At least they couldn't run very fast in their tight jeans and engineer boots.

Rumor had it the ninth grade gym teacher was big on running laps, which, compared to Mr. Swenson's classes, didn't sound half bad, though some of us were starting to wonder if we could hold out long enough to make it into ninth grade. There were only so many times you could get your mother to write a note saying you were sick and should be excused from gym. When I tried to look on the bright side, I'd never gotten such good grades in a gym class—but then, everybody else did too, at least everybody who was smart enough to show up and keep their mouths shut.

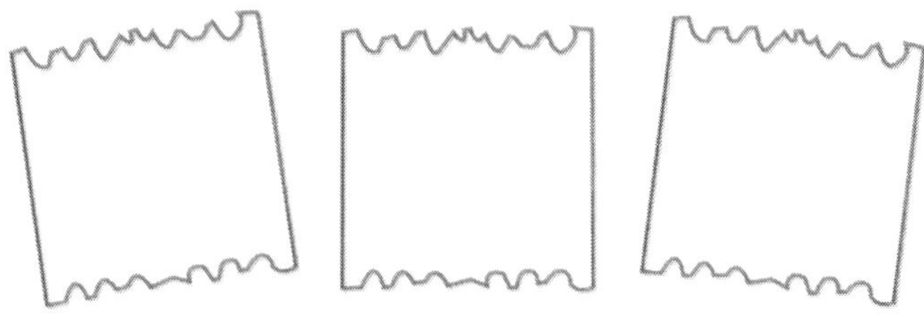

Out of Control

Our eighth grade biology teacher should have known better if anybody should. One day she decided we'd all have to stand beside our desks when she called on us to answer questions, as if she didn't know about the boners the boys could get even at the worst of times. Most of the boys found a way to slide from their desks and half crouch or hold a book in front of them, thankful the girls in that class never seemed to notice and hating that gray-faced teacher more and more each day.

English was another matter, with a sweet new first-year teacher who thought she could control the boys by ringing this little bell she kept on her desk. More than once we made her cry with our rowdiness—even if we liked her, we just couldn't seem to help ourselves. Maybe it was because that class came right after biology for most of us. Maybe it was because it was just about the only class in junior high where we could let off some steam. There she'd stand, so young and small and pretty, trying to ring the bell we'd stopped up with bubblegum, and all of us knowing we couldn't shut up until there were tears.

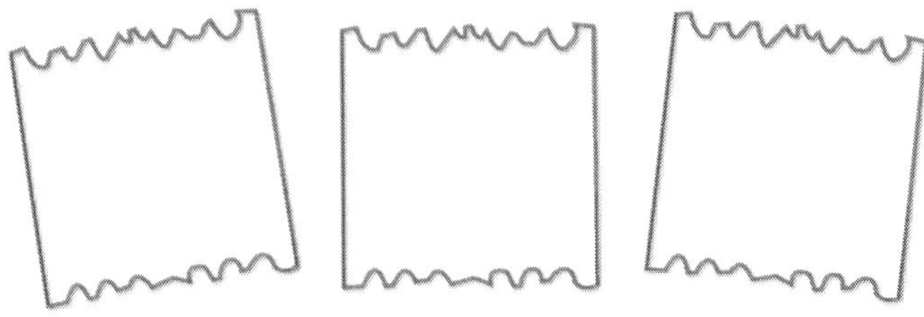

Fashion Statement

During the winter of eighth grade my friend Pete surprised me by showing up at school in a pair of pale green corduroy pants. A lot of the other guys were wearing pastel cords and shirts, even pink ones. When I asked my father if I could get a pair too, he just looked at me like I was someone he didn't know. I didn't ask again, but it wasn't very long before my mother came home from shopping downtown with a pair of cords she'd found on sale somewhere—baby blue, she called them, grinning at me. But I did need some pants and, well, if that's what I really wanted . . . . She just worried about my being able to keep them clean. I couldn't, of course, any more than those white buck shoes I had to wear for band, which the hoods loved to stomp on with their engineer boots. But even some of the hoods were wearing pink dress shirts with their jeans, sleeves rolled tight against their muscles. Most of the time, my blue cords were in the dirty clothes hamper because I'd sat in something or spilled something or smeared ink from my ballpoint pen.

When I thought about it, for as long as I could remember, the girls seemed to wear the same kinds of clothes, like matching skirt and sweater outfits or fluffy white socks and penny loafers. But I couldn't remember the boys doing that—except, of course, all of us had some kind of imitation ducktail hairdos. The hoods were the only ones who could carry off the real thing.

When the warm weather finally came, we all wore our short-sleeve shirts with the sleeves rolled up, and some of the guys showed up in chino pants with a little buckled belt just above the back pockets—which, more than anything else, was good for grabbing or even ripping off. Sometimes I had to wonder who dreamed up all of those clothes and styles and why they got so popular so quickly. I also wondered whether kids at other schools were dressing just like we did, or kids in other cities, or even other states. What if everybody all over the country was wearing the same thing? And then I'd start thinking about why we all had to do it, especially when what we were wearing was stupid or uncomfortable. Deep down, I knew I looked ridiculous in my powder blue cords, especially to my father, who never admitted to dressing like that when he was my age. My mother said it was because he grew up too poor to afford things that were in fashion, though since her father was a doctor she pretty much got whatever clothes she wanted. She couldn't do that any more, of course, and maybe that was one reason she bought me those cords in the first place.

When the warm weather came and everyone stopped wearing cords, I had a feeling we'd all be wearing something very different in the fall. And sometimes, when I'd see those powder blue cords hanging in my closet and wonder if I'd ever be able to wear them again, I'd be glad my mother didn't have to wash them every other day any more. At least I knew she appreciated that.

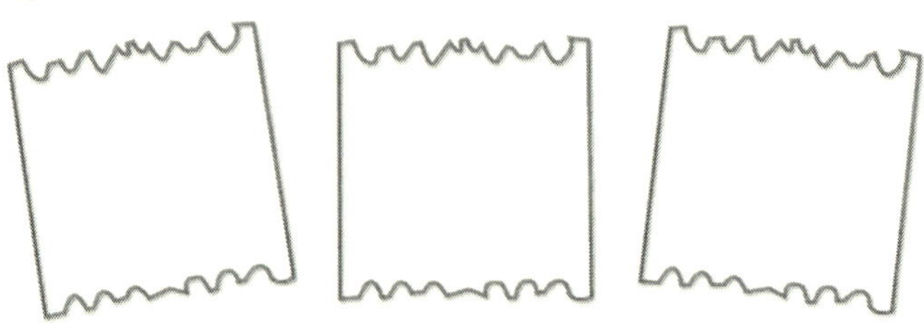

Auld Lang Syne

I didn't find out about celebrating New Year's Eve until I was six or seven and my parents got invited to a party. By the time the babysitter arrived they were all dressed up. In his suit and tie, my father looked pretty much like he always did when he went to work, but I'd never seen my mother in such a nice dress—or wearing glittery jewelry, or smelling so good, or seeming so happy. The only thing she told me about the party was that there would be dancing, and what a good dancer my father was. Dancing or not, I wanted more than anything to go with them, but she just smiled and said I'd have to wait till I got a lot older. One day I'd have plenty of parties to attend.

I don't remember my parents ever going to a party again and it wasn't for a few more years that I got to stay up till midnight with them and have eggnog and cookies and watch TV. One year my father even went out on the front steps at midnight and fired his shotgun into the air. There were firecrackers going off all over the neighborhood, car horns honking, and people shouting. I couldn't wait till I was old enough to go to do stuff like that.

By the time I got to eighth grade and could start thinking about going to parties, I'd suddenly become very popular as a babysitter, probably because I was the only teenager left in the neighborhood. Even before Christmas, several people called and asked if I could stay with their kids on New Year's Eve, but I ended up going where I usually did, to the Ashbys across the street.

It was pretty easy watching their little kids, especially since they were asleep most of the time I was there and I could just lie on the couch and watch movies on TV. When it got close to midnight and I started hearing the firecrackers and horns, I knew I had to do something to celebrate, but the only thing that came to me was to call my parents and hope they'd still be up so I could wish them wish them a happy New Year. At least we didn't have to worry where to find each other.

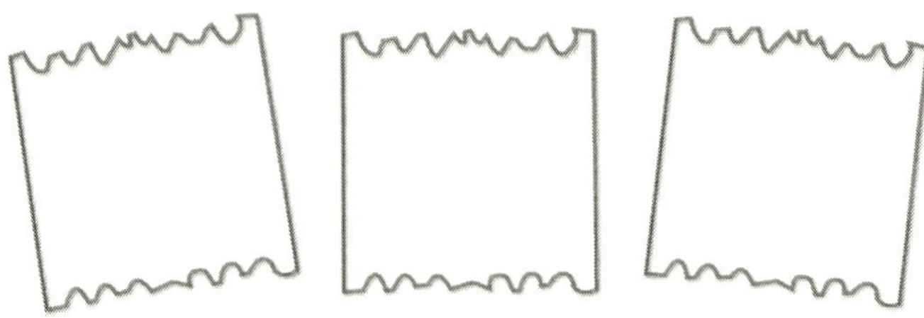

The Music Scene

For awhile in junior high, kids divided themselves into two big groups—the followers of Elvis and the Pat Boone crowd. Most of the clean-cut kids wore Pat Boone buttons, and while I had bought Elvis records and listened to them constantly, it pained me to be in a group with so many people I didn't like, especially the hoods. There were a couple of black kids in the Elvis group but most of them kept to themselves and listened to Bo Diddley or Chuck Berry or the Coasters and some other groups I'd never heard of. My friend Pete bought some of those records and I had to admit they were every bit as good as Elvis, whose songs were starting to show up on *Your Hit Parade* on TV, although that program's idea of rock and roll was pretty pathetic. In band we even played a way-too-slow version of *Rock Around the Clock* at the fall concert.

My parents never paid a lot of attention to what I listened to as long I didn't blast the volume on the record player, though I knew that most grownups could get pretty upset about any kind of rock and roll music. So, I played my records when nobody else was around, or I went over to Pete's house when his parents were at work and we blasted Bo Diddley or the Coasters and sang along and danced around till we got dizzy and fell down screaming and laughing. We were never quite sure what we were laughing at—just that we had to do it as often and as loudly as we possibly could.

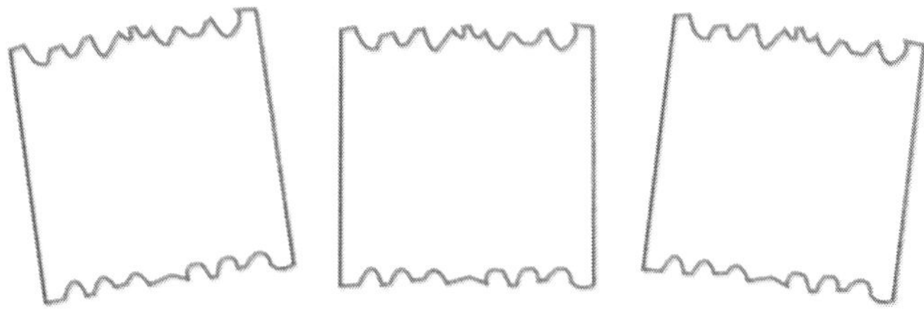

Dynamic Tension

A lot of the comic books I read had ads for the Charles Atlas body-building course which was based on something called Dynamic Tension. They always pictured some skinny guy who was getting pushed around by muscular guys till he started using the Charles Atlas method and came back a few weeks later with his own huge muscles and pushed those other guys around while the girls marveled. Even if I knew I'd never order that book—or whatever it was—it was somehow reassuring to think that maybe it was there as a possibility.

When school started in ninth grade this kid named George who used to be fat and dumpy showed up looking like one of those "After" guys in the comic book ads. It turns out he'd worked hard on Dynamic Tension all summer. From then on, whenever you'd see George he'd be rolling his shirt sleeves up a little tighter, practicing his cool walk down the hall, combing his ducktail in the reflection of every glass door. Eventually, we heard he was flunking out of school because he didn't pay attention to anything anymore, but worse than that, he'd become one of the bullies pushing the seventh-graders around and forcing them to cough up their lunch money. One day in the locker room someone reminded George that it wasn't very long ago that he was the one getting pushed around. "Ain't that a shame," George said, right after he'd doubled that guy up with a punch to the belly. Then George strutted off to Industrial Arts, flexing those muscles for all he was worth.

The Hard Way

A couple of times a week there'd be a fight after school. We seldom knew why, caught in the circle of shouts and eyes as everyone gathered around two bodies clenched and rolling on the gravel playground. Except for split lips and shiners, no one really got hurt. Most days the boys who'd been fighting would simply walk away, arms draped around each other as if they'd suddenly learned something secret and become best friends—until the next time it got started, which it always did, leaving the rest of us to wonder if it was ever going to be our turn.

Once in awhile, it was even two girls who fought, and just like the boys they eventually walked away arm in arm, as if nothing ever happened—except for a cut cheek or a messed-up hairdo. It seemed that just about anything could get a fight started, and the best thing was to try to look inconspicuous and keep your head down. After all, this was only junior high. One day we'd graduate and get to go to high school—the place some of us didn't even want to think about.

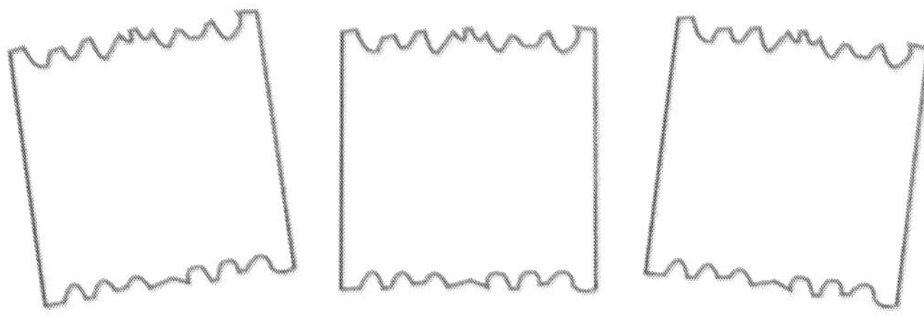

Hoods

If there were a lot of kids in junior high who liked to dress and act like hoods, there was only one real one. His name was Kenny and it was rumored that he was given the choice of going back to junior high or to the state reformatory. Even if he was a couple of years older than the rest of us, he came back to school—in his black leather jacket and motorcycle boots with the half-moon cleats, with his ballpoint pen tattoo and five o'clock shadow, and maybe with that long switchblade everybody said he must be hiding somewhere. Before school started in the morning we'd see him at the little store across the street, smoking and drinking coffee with a group of his followers who did their best to look and act just like Kenny, swearing and spitting and combing their greasy hair.

The only class I had with Kenny was typing, which was something we both were terrible at, and maybe that's why he always left me alone, the two of us hunting and pecking in the back row, where the teacher often came and stood behind Kenny, which made him jam the keys even more. One day, when the teacher had said out loud that Kenny was hopeless, we all watched Kenny's face getting redder and redder, and finally, when the teacher went back to the front of the room just as the bell was about to ring, Kenny took his typewriter to the open third-story window and pitched it out. Then he just ambled out the back door of the classroom, fishing a cigarette from his shirt pocket as he went.

We never saw Kenny after that, though we heard plenty of rumors—

that he'd stolen a car and shot it out with the cops over on Clinton Avenue, that he'd stolen a beer truck and driven it to Central High, three blocks away, and passed out bottles of beer to the high school kids after school. What we heard got more and more ridiculous, to the point I began to wonder if I really saw him putt that cigarette in his mouth or throw that typewriter out the window, or if he just left it on the sill. I didn't suppose we'd ever learn the truth about Kenny, except that we all were terrified of him and attracted to him at the same time, even the most stuck-up of the girls. We also knew that the stories about him were going to keep on growing—Kenny out there cruising in his stolen wheels, one turn ahead of the cops, giving the finger to every hopeless case he passed.

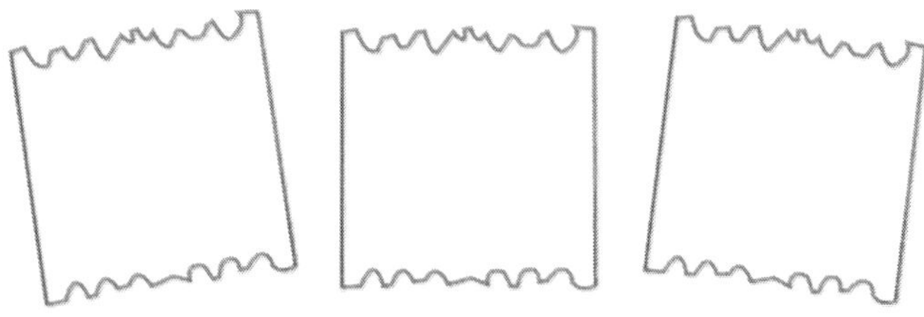

Love Me Tender

The only place in our house that I could play my music was on the record player that was part of the TV console in the living room. Most of the time that was no problem, but one afternoon when my little sister was staying over at one of her friend's and my father was away on a trip, my grandmother and Aunt Molly came over for dinner, and when my aunt saw some of my record jackets on the floor by the record player she started in on what a bad influence that Elvis Presley hoodlum was, reminding me that when Elvis was on Ed Sullivan they didn't even show him below the waist, and what kind of name was *Elvis*, anyway? My grandmother, who had no idea who Elvis Presley was, had to agree with her about how terrible the music was that kids were listening to, and then she started telling the story about when she was a girl and learned to love the best kind of music there was by singing in the church choir. When I couldn't stand listening to her anymore, I lied and told her I'd read somewhere that Elvis sang in the church choir when he was a boy, too, and then she said that if I was so smart maybe I could play them a record of Elvis Presley singing church music. Well, I didn't have a record like that, though I guessed she might somehow like this sappy, sentimental song called *Old Shep*, which was the worst Elvis song I'd ever heard. I was flabbergasted when she said she liked it even if it wasn't a hymn, and Aunt Molly said it was such a beautiful song that I should play it again, which I did, followed by *Love*

Me Tender, the only other Elvis song I could think of that they might possibly like. Sure enough, I had to play that one again too.

Since it wasn't long before dinnertime, my mother was in the kitchen and Grandma and Aunt Molly were having highballs, and I probably should have known better than playing any music at all, because they kept asking me to repeat those same two songs over and over, and pretty soon Aunt Molly started crying because Elvis was such a sweet boy to love his dog like that and his mother, too, though I didn't know where she got that idea about his mother. But I did know it wouldn't be long before they got started on what kind of a boy *I* was. The only thing that saved me was my mother coming into the living room to have her own highball, even though she started getting teary about *Old Shep*, too, and then about the dog she had when she and my father lived in Montana before I was even born. And there was this dog back in their hometown, a little Scottie or something like that, and pretty soon my aunt and grandmother were in a big argument over what kind of dog it was. I don't think any of them even noticed when I turned off the record player and slipped upstairs to my room, knowing for certain that dinner was going to be really late that evening, and if the subject of Elvis Presley ever came up again I was going to get slaughtered when they compared me to such a sweet boy as that.

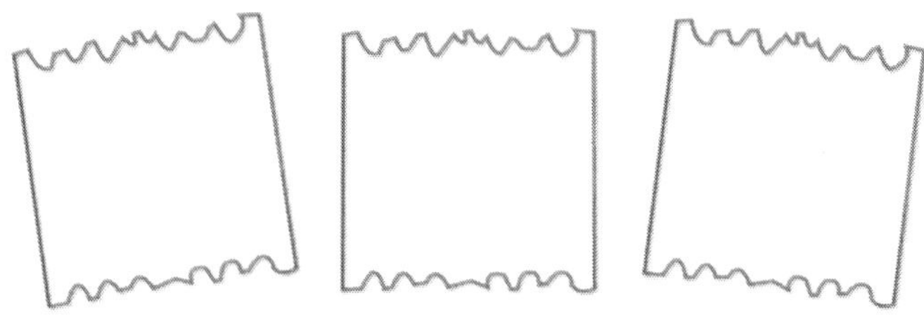

Motorcycles

There weren't any real motorcycles in our neighborhood, but Dennis Wiley had some kind of motorbike he'd reconstructed from spare parts. At least that's what he said—and who could doubt it? His skin was gray, his clothes all stained with grease. And so what if he was flunking out? He worked on that machine for hours each day. Like our parents, we all believed he'd kill himself one day—we'd been warned about motorcycles, about knives and cigarettes, too, which were Dennis' other passions. Up and down the alley every evening, Chesterfield dangling from his lip, he'd cruise while we shot baskets, emptied trash, and walked our dogs. "Try a butt," he'd call out, laughing as he rode down the alley in a cloud of blue-gray smoke..

And then one day there was a girl on the back of Dennis Wiley's bike— and not just any girl. Her name was Mary Kay. We knew it by heart, by the times we'd walked past her house just to hope she'd be home noticing us. Then there was another girl we'd never seen before, and then another. He'd left the block. He'd even left the neighborhood, and all we could do was stand there helplessly and watch. "Try one," he'd call, and we'd just stare at each other, not quite sure what he meant, but sure we probably couldn't. Not that way, at any rate. Not with Mary Kay or anyone else with eyes like hers. And not in this bewildering life.

End of a Season

My father said he was always a New York Yankee fan. He'd talk about Yogi Berra or Phil Rizzuto like they were members of his family. For some reason, maybe to be different from him, I decided to like the Brooklyn Dodgers—Gil Hodges, Duke Snider, Peewee Reese, Jackie Robinson. I knew all the players.

During the years we lived in the apartment house it seemed like just about every fall the Yankees and Dodgers would end up playing in the World Series, and every year the Yankees would win and I'd lose the bet I'd made with my father. Even if it was nothing more than doing the dishes or cleaning my room, it made me really frustrated, especially because it seemed like my father knew something important that I didn't. Don't get so down, he's say. The Dodgers are a good team—it takes a lot to be second-best, you know, and they'll probably be back in the Series again next year. I knew they probably would—and that they'd end up losing again, too. The one time my father and I were in agreement was the year the New York Giants beat the Cleveland Indians in the World Series, thanks to Willie Mays—who'd even played for a short time for our Millers, a Triple-A farm club for the Giants.

Not till I was in junior high did the Dodgers finally end up beating the Yankees, but by then both my father and I seemed to have lost a lot of interest in the World Series—we didn't even get around to making a bet. Mostly, I was hanging out with my friend Pete at his house, or with other friends, talking a lot about what high school was going to be like. My father and I did watch part of one game on TV together, which Johnny Podres pitched and won for the Dodgers. Afterwards, when I asked my father how he liked being second-best for a change, he just smiled and said we'd have to wait till next year, wouldn't we, when things just might be a lot different. I knew that he was probably right—and that he wasn't only talking about baseball, either.

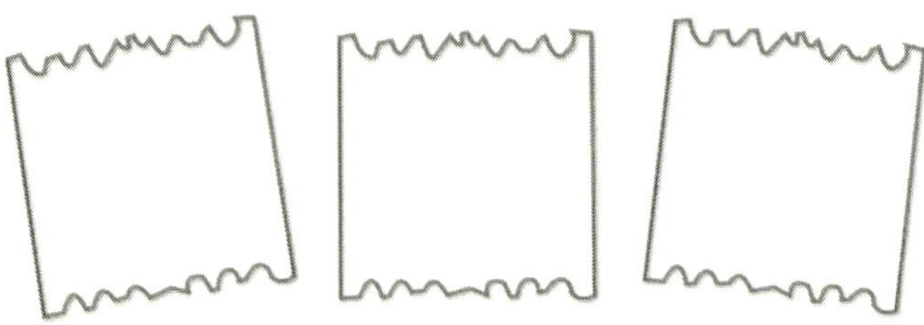

Into the Sunset

I can't remember when my father first told me that he'd taken a new job and we'd be moving at the end of the summer. This time, however, it wouldn't be as simple as across town or even out to the suburbs, where a lot of families in our neighborhood had started moving. This time it would be to another city, too far away for me to imagine, which is probably why it took a long time to sink in. The only thing that got me excited was the thought of living in a place with a major league baseball team.

My father said the time we had left before the move was really going to fly, and as usual he was right. All of a sudden it was the Sunday before the van was due to come, and my friend Stevie's parents invited our family to their house out by the airport for a backyard cookout—to give us a break from all the sorting and packing. After we'd eaten our burgers and potato salad, Stevie's mom suggested that he and I walk over to the neighborhood movie theater for the matinee of *Oklahoma*, which would be a lot more interesting than sitting around the backyard with the grownups and little kids.

I hadn't heard of the movie, though I guessed it was some kind of western, which might be fun to see. But when we got settled into our seats, ready for a good gunfight or cavalry charge, the movie turned out to be a really stupid musical which both of us had a hard time sitting through.

A couple of hours later, when we were in the car and pulling away from Stevie and his family standing in their driveway and waving, I could tell that my mother had been crying. But she also kept saying not to worry, that things were going to work out in the end. Maybe that was when it finally hit me that it would be a long time before I'd get to go to a movie—even a bad one— with a friend like Stevie. And then, I couldn't stop thinking there were a lot of other people I was probably never going to see again.

ONLY 1200 STAMPS
FILL THIS

Acknowledgements

Grateful acknowledgement to reprint some of these works from their initial appearances in the following periodicals and other sources, sometimes in partially different form:

Another Chicago Magazine, Flash Flash Click, Great River Review, Poetry Now, Sentence: A Journal of Prose Poetics, The Shining Times, Sidewalks, Spoon River Quarterly, and *Verve.*

Many of these pieces first appeared in *The Weird* Kid (1983) and *Late Night Calls* (1992) by Mark Vinz, both published by New Rivers Press.

Some pieces were also reprinted in The Evergreen Reader program, Minnesota Humanities Commission, *Stiller's Pond: New Fiction from the Upper Midwest,* Enlarged Second Edition, ed. by Jonis Agee, Roger Blakely, and Susan Welch (New Rivers Press, 1991), *Stirring the Deep: The Poetry of Mark Vinz* by Thom Tammaro (Spoon River Poetry Press, 1989), *Identity Lessons: Contemporary Writing about Learning to Be American,* ed. Maria Mazziotti Gillan and Jennifer Gillan, (Penguin Books, 1999), and *Nothing to Declare: A Guide to the Flash Sequence,* ed. Robert Alexander, Eric Braun, and Debra Marquart (White Pine Press, 2016).

Special thanks for their advice and encouragement to Lin Enger, Tom Hansen, Yahya Frederickson, Kevin Zepper, Jay Meek, Thom Tammaro, Joe Richardson, and as always, to my wife Betsy Vinz.

About the Author

Mark Vinz was born in North Dakota, grew up in Minneapolis and the Kansas City area, and taught in the English department of Minnesota University Moorhead for 39 years, where he was also editor of Dacotah Territory Press and the first coordinator of MSUM's Master of Fine Arts in Creative Writing program. His poems, stories, and essays have appeared in numerous magazines and anthologies, and he is the author of several books of poems, most recently *The Work Is All* and *Permanent Record*. He is also the co-editor of literature anthologies such as *Inheriting the Land: Contemporary Voices from the Midwest* and *The Party Train: A Collection of North American Prose Poetry*.

Other accomplishments include three Minnesota Book Awards, six PEN Syndicated Fiction awards, a fellowship in poetry from the National Endowment for the Arts, and the 2014 Kay Sexton Award "in recognition of long-standing dedication and outstanding work in fostering books, reading, and literary activity in Minnesota."

About New Rivers Press

New Rivers Press emerged from a drafty Massachusetts barn in winter 1968. Intent on publishing work by new and emerging poets, founder C. W. "Bill" Truesdale labored for weeks over an old Chandler & Price letterpress to publish three hundred fifty copies of Margaret Randall's collection, *So Many Rooms Has a House But One Roof.*

Nearly four hundred titles later, New Rivers, a non-profit and now teaching press based since 2001 at Minnesota State University Moorhead, has remained true to Bill's goal of publishing the best new literature—poetry and prose—from new, emerging, and established writers.

New Rivers Press authors range in age from twenty to eighty-nine. They include a silversmith, a carpenter, a geneticist, a monk, a tree-trimmer, and a rock musician. They hail from cities such as Christchurch, Honolulu, New Orleans, New York City, Northfield (Minnesota), and Prague.

Charles Baxter, one of the first authors with New Rivers, calls the press "the hidden backbone of the American literary tradition." Continuing this tradition, in 1981 New Rivers began to sponsor the Minnesota Voices Project (now called Many Voices Project) competition. It is one of the oldest literary competitions in the United States, bringing recognition and attention to emerging writers. Other New Rivers publications include the *American Fiction Series, the American Poetry Series, New Rivers Abroad,* and the *Electronic Book Series.*

Please visit our website **newriverspress.com** for more information.